WORLD
HISTORY SERIES

The Rise and Fall of the Soviet Union

Titles in the World History Series

WORLD
HISTORY SERIES ▪▪▪

The Rise and Fall of the Soviet Union

by
John R. Matthews

Lucent Books, P.O. Box 289011, San Diego, CA 92198-9011

Library of Congress Cataloging-in-Publication Data

Matthews, John R., 1937–
    The Rise and Fall of the Soviet Union / by John R. Matthews.
        p.   cm.—(World history series)
    Includes bibliographical references and index.
    Summary: Discusses the history of the Soviet Union, from the revolution of 1917, through the Lenin and Stalin eras and the rule of such leaders as Khrushchev, Brezhnev, and Gorbachev, up to the formal dissolution of the Soviet Union in 1991.
    ISBN 1-56006-567-2 (lib. bdg. : alk. paper)
    1. Soviet Union—Juvenile literature. [1. Soviet Union.] I. Title. II. Series.
DK266.M349 2000
947—dc21   99-34059
                                                    CIP

Contents

Foreword

Each year on the first day of school, nearly every history teacher faces the task of explaining why his or her students should study history. One logical answer to this question is that exploring what happened in our past explains how the things we often take for granted—our customs, ideas, and institutions—came to be. As statesman and historian Winston Churchill put it, "Every nation or group of nations has its own tale to tell. Knowledge of the trials and struggles is necessary to all who would comprehend the problems, perils, challenges, and opportunities which confront us today." Thus, a study of history puts modern ideas and institutions in perspective. For example, though the founders of the United States were talented and creative thinkers, they clearly did not invent the concept of democracy. Instead, they adapted some democratic ideas that had originated in ancient Greece and with which the Romans, the British, and others had experimented. An exploration of these cultures, then, reveals their very real connection to us through institutions that continue to shape our daily lives.

Another reason often given for studying history is the idea that lessons exist in the past from which contemporary societies can benefit and learn. This idea, although controversial, has always been an intriguing one for historians. Those who agree that society can benefit from the past often quote philosopher George Santayana's famous statement, "Those who cannot remember the past are condemned to repeat it." Historians who subscribe to Santayana's philosophy believe that, for example, studying the events that led up to the major world wars or other significant historical events would allow society to chart a different and more favorable course in the future.

Just as difficult as convincing students to realize the importance of studying history is the search for useful and interesting supplementary materials that present historical events in a context that can be easily understood. The volumes in Lucent Books' World History Series attempt to present a broad, balanced, and penetrating view of the march of history. Ancient Egypt's important wars and rulers, for example, are presented against the rich and colorful backdrop of Egyptian religious, social, and cultural developments. The series engages the reader by enhancing historical events with these cultural contexts. For example, in *Ancient Greece,* the text covers the role of women in that society. Slavery is discussed in *The Roman Empire,* as well as how slaves earned their freedom. The numerous and varied aspects of every-day life in these and other societies are explored in each volume of the series. Additionally, the series covers the major political, cultural, and philosophical ideas as the torch of civilization is passed from ancient Mesopotamia and Egypt, through Greece, Rome, Medieval Europe, and other world cultures, to the modern day.

The material in the series is formatted in a thorough, precise, and organized manner. Each volume offers the reader a comprehensive and clearly written overview of an important historical event or period. The topic under discussion is placed in a broad, historical context. For example, *The Italian Renaissance* begins with a discussion of the High Middle Ages and the loss of central control that allowed certain Italian cities to develop artistically. The book ends by looking forward to the Reformation and interpreting the societal changes that grew out of the Renaissance. Thus, students are not only involved in an historical era, but also enveloped by the events leading up to that era and the events following it.

One important and unique feature in the World History Series is the primary and secondary source quotations that richly supplement each volume. These quotes are useful in a number of ways. First, they allow students access to sources they would not normally be exposed to because of the difficulty and obscurity of the original source. The quotations range from interesting anecdotes to far-sighted cultural perspectives and are drawn from historical witnesses both past and present. Second, the quotes demonstrate how and where historians themselves derive their information on the past as they strive to reach a consensus on historical events. Lastly, all of the quotes are footnoted, familiarizing students with the citation process and allowing them to verify quotes and/or look up the original source if the quote piques their interest.

Finally, the books in the World History Series provide a detailed launching point for further research. Each book contains a bibliography specifically geared toward student research. A second, annotated bibliography introduces students to all the sources the author consulted when compiling the book. A chronology of important dates gives students an overview, at a glance, of the topic covered. Where applicable, a glossary of terms is included.

In short, the series is designed not only to acquaint readers with the basics of history, but also to make them aware that their lives are a part of an ongoing human saga. Perhaps they will then come to the same realization as famed historian Arnold Toynbee. In his monumental work, *A Study of History,* he wrote about becoming aware of history flowing through him in a mighty current, and of his own life "welling like a wave in the flow of this vast tide."

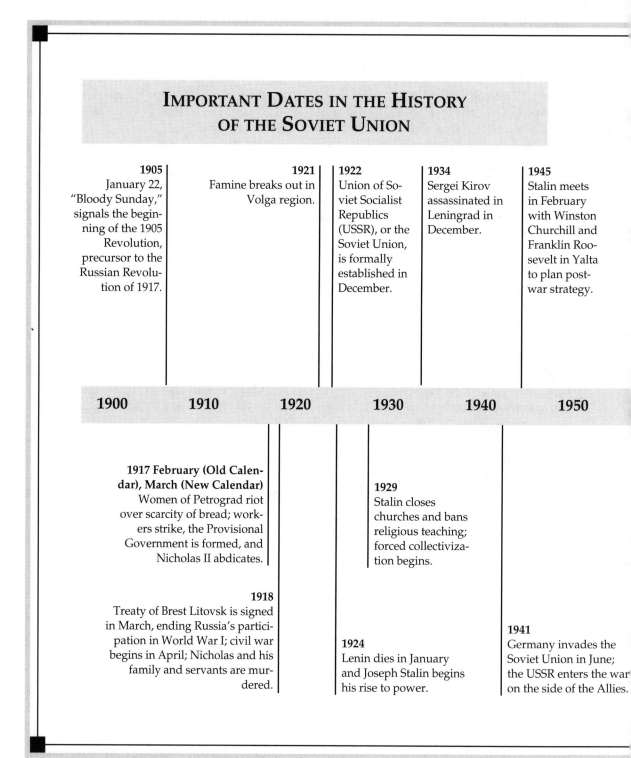

IMPORTANT DATES IN THE HISTORY OF THE SOVIET UNION

1905
January 22, "Bloody Sunday," signals the beginning of the 1905 Revolution, precursor to the Russian Revolution of 1917.

1921
Famine breaks out in Volga region.

1922
Union of Soviet Socialist Republics (USSR), or the Soviet Union, is formally established in December.

1934
Sergei Kirov assassinated in Leningrad in December.

1945
Stalin meets in February with Winston Churchill and Franklin Roosevelt in Yalta to plan postwar strategy.

1900   1910   1920   1930   1940   1950

1917 February (Old Calendar), March (New Calendar)
Women of Petrograd riot over scarcity of bread; workers strike, the Provisional Government is formed, and Nicholas II abdicates.

1918
Treaty of Brest Litovsk is signed in March, ending Russia's participation in World War I; civil war begins in April; Nicholas and his family and servants are murdered.

1929
Stalin closes churches and bans religious teaching; forced collectivization begins.

1924
Lenin dies in January and Joseph Stalin begins his rise to power.

1941
Germany invades the Soviet Union in June; the USSR enters the war on the side of the Allies.

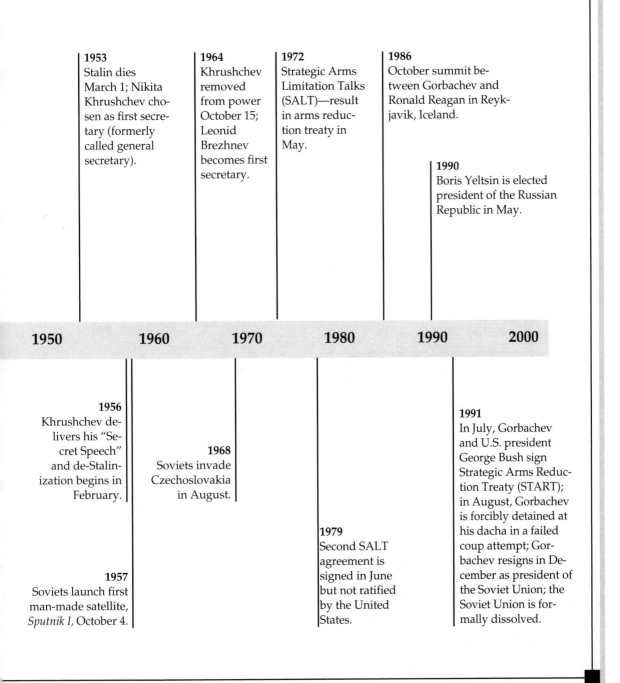

1953
Stalin dies March 1; Nikita Khrushchev chosen as first secretary (formerly called general secretary).

1964
Khrushchev removed from power October 15; Leonid Brezhnev becomes first secretary.

1972
Strategic Arms Limitation Talks (SALT)—result in arms reduction treaty in May.

1986
October summit between Gorbachev and Ronald Reagan in Reykjavik, Iceland.

1990
Boris Yeltsin is elected president of the Russian Republic in May.

1950　1960　1970　1980　1990　2000

1956
Khrushchev delivers his "Secret Speech" and de-Stalinization begins in February.

1968
Soviets invade Czechoslovakia in August.

1957
Soviets launch first man-made satellite, *Sputnik I*, October 4.

1979
Second SALT agreement is signed in June but not ratified by the United States.

1991
In July, Gorbachev and U.S. president George Bush sign Strategic Arms Reduction Treaty (START); in August, Gorbachev is forcibly detained at his dacha in a failed coup attempt; Gorbachev resigns in December as president of the Soviet Union; the Soviet Union is formally dissolved.

On the Eve of the Revolution

When the Russian Revolution began in 1917, no one—not even its most ardent supporters—correctly predicted the outcome. Before the end of that fateful year, Czar Nicholas II, the hereditary ruler of Russia, would be arrested. The following year, during the civil war fought to deter-

Czar Nicholas II, pictured here with three of his daughters, under arrest after the abdication.

mine whether or not the newly installed Socialist government would survive, Nicholas and his family—the czarina Alexandra and the couple's son and four daughters, along with their servants—were brutally murdered. The new government, whose leaders called themselves communists, would begin a seventy-four-year-long series of disasters from which the country has yet to recover.

PRELUDE TO AN UPRISING

The Russian Revolution was rooted in the preceding century, a time of peasant revolts and agitation by radicals calling for revolution. In response to this unrest, the imperial government made attempts at reform, but often these efforts were more impressive on paper than in fact. For example, serfdom, a remnant of feudalism that consigned millions to virtual slavery as peasants, was abolished in 1861, but with freedom came unwelcome costs to the former serfs. Now they were required to purchase the land they worked on, and the government ordered them to make payments to their former masters over a forty-nine-year period. John Bergamini, biographer of the Romanov dynasty,

PRECURSORS TO REVOLUTION

The restlessness of both factory workers and peasants and the social turmoil created by both industrialization and agriculture reform after the freeing of the serfs in 1861 were important factors contributing to the revolution. Helene Carrere d'Encausse, a political scientist at the University of Paris, describes the peasants' plight in the years leading up to the revolution in her book Lenin: Revolution and Power.

"At the turn of the century, the great problem of the Russian empire was land. The peasants represented 80 per cent of the population [of about 159 million in 1913], and the land on which they lived could not produce enough to feed them. In 1861, the agrarian reform had abolished serfdom and given the peasants the right to buy land. Many of them, too poor to avail themselves of this opportunity, passed their right on, while others burdened themselves with permanent debt. The countryside contained landless peasants, owners of tiny plots of land, richer peasants, great landowners. The reform maintained cultivation in common [a holdover from serfdom]. . . . Preserved because the autocracy thought that it was a stabilizing factor in the countryside, [this communal practice] paralysed the activity of the most dynamic peasants and hampered the progress of agriculture."

Nicholas's family, observed that on hearing about their freedom, an "audience of ex-serfs actually burst out laughing when told of the forty-nine-year burden placed on them."[1] The periodic peasant revolts following emancipation of the serfs, along with a growing movement among educated elites for some form of participation in the national government, created an atmosphere of destabilization that culminated in two revolutions early in the following century. The second of these revolutions successfully overthrew the monarchy.

Together with peasant unrest and radicalization of the intelligentsia, something else very important was happening: Industrialization had belatedly reached Russia. However, such a vast, backward country could not convert itself to a truly industrialized state in a short time despite such mammoth projects as the construction of the Trans-Siberian Railway; consequently, the coming of industry had little direct impact on the vast majority of the Russian people. Nevertheless, the small but growing number of industrial workers presented a challenge to the elite

Peasant unrest and revolt led to two revolutions, the second of which was a successful overthrow of the monarchy.

radicals. According to cultural historian Joel Carmichael, the radicals "concentrated their attention on the industrial working-class as the sole channel through which a transformation of society could be effected."[2]

Russia's introduction to the Industrial Revolution did not occur as a result of initiatives by homegrown entrepreneurs. Instead the government invited foreign financial partners to help build an industrial empire that was to be paid for at least partly by taxes on the peasants' exported produce. Thus massive industrial plants were built in an effort to catapult Russia into the modern world.

This headlong lunge into industrialization resulted in social changes that favored the ideas of the radical intelligentsia seeking revolution. These revolutionary groups were led by educated intellectuals and sympathetic members of the upper classes who were fascinated by socialist ideas circulating throughout Europe. The most influential ideas about socialism were propounded by nineteenth-century German philosopher Karl Marx (1818–1883).

SOCIALISM: A RADICAL EXPERIMENT

Karl Marx believed that the development of civilized societies was driven primarily by economic factors. He thought this development would occur in inevitable stages; before socialism could be achieved, a capitalist stage would have to be developed. His definition of capitalism was simply that the means of production (factories, railroads, retail outlets, etc.) were owned by a few "capitalists," who accumulated profits from the labor of workers. Thus a handful of rich capitalists would eventually own all the capital of the country, and would demand more and more work from its workers for less pay. This would lead to widespread unrest and revolt by the workers, who would overthrow the capitalists as well as the government that supported the capitalistic system. The final stage would be the

Karl Marx believed socialism would be achieved in Russia.

development of communism, in which workers would rule themselves cooperatively within their communities, and the state would cease to exist.

Marx's philosophy was debated throughout Europe during the latter years of the nineteenth century and especially in Russia, where unrest created by poverty and oppression was growing. This unrest would explode in revolution in 1905.

THE 1905 REVOLUTION

In 1905 a revolution broke out that was in a way a dress rehearsal for the 1917 revolution, meaning that it did not succeed. In an atmosphere of rising unrest, the czar instituted oppressive measures, such as restrictions on the press and on public assembly, which further energized the radicals.

On January 22, 1905, a day that soon became known as Bloody Sunday, government troops fired on peaceful demonstrators gathered in Saint Petersburg, the Russian capital, to press for reform. Bloody Sunday inspired further demonstrations and strikes. A worried Czar Nicholas responded by agreeing to limited reform. He established an elected assembly, the Duma, to participate in lawmaking and share government power. This move blunted the hopes of the radicals, who wanted not reforms but the removal of the czar and the establishment of a socialist government.

Unfortunately, Nicholas did not like sharing authority with the Duma, nor did he like the legislation coming out of it. He therefore dissolved the first Duma session in 1906, the second in 1907, and the third in 1912. In a state of political impasse, he resumed totalitarian rule. Popular hostility, as represented by both the Duma and reform groups, simmered throughout the period from the 1905 uprising until the start of World War I in 1914.

WORLD WAR I

Russia entered World War I in 1914 on the side of France and Britain to oppose territorial aggression in the Balkans by Austria-Hungary and Germany. At first the Russian people seemed to back the war effort, but the momentum generated by early battlefield successes dissipated. As Daniel Diller, in his excellent short history of the Soviet Union, explains, "a series of military disasters on the German front dashed morale [and there was] an excessively high rate of Russian casualties."[3]

Russian troops were recruited mostly from the peasant class, and the resulting drain on agricultural workers on Russia's primitive farms led to food shortages. The civilian sector was particularly hard hit because produce was diverted to feed the troops at the front. In February 1917 bread riots erupted in the capital, now named Petrograd, which in turn inspired strikes and demonstrations against the war.

To Nicholas the war effort was central to the survival of Russia, and the ruler spent much time visiting his troops at the front. In his absence, his stay-at-home ministers ignored the urgent messages coming from the streets, occupying themselves instead with palace intrigues. As a result, no one in government was prepared to deal with the growing unrest due to food shortages. The unrest, especially the bread riots, served as a signal to summon the revolutionary forces that had been quietly preparing for this opportunity since the failure of the 1905 revolution.

1 The Revolution of 1917

The first shocks of the revolution of 1917 were felt in Petrograd in February. It was the third year of World War I, and food had become so scarce that normally law-abiding people rioted in the streets. These bread riots in turn inspired other protests, including massive demonstrations and strikes by factory workers and soldiers exhausted by the demands of war.

THE BREAD RIOTS

Nicholas and his ministers initially dismissed the bread riots as another series of uprisings that could be put down, just as similar disturbances had been dispelled in the past. They were wrong. The riots not only failed to subside as expected, but grew more explosive by the day. Jonathan Sanders, a historian of the revolution, describes the mood of the people: "It took little sophistication for those fed up with inequities to affix blame. Placards proclaiming DOWN WITH THE MONARCHY appeared."[4]

The troops assigned to discipline the rioters were loyal to the czar; when critics of the monarchy turned violent, some

Two soldiers who ignored orders to fire their weapons against their own people joined the ranks of demonstrators during the bread riots.

units responded as instructed by their officers and fired into the crowds. Many soldiers, however, reluctant to fire on their own people, simply refused to shoot their countrymen. Other troops ignored orders and joined the ranks of demonstrators.

Historian William Henry Chamberlin describes how a group of Cossacks, elite cavalrymen from southern Russia, resolved their dilemma of divided loyalty: "A Cossack squadron rode off, amid loud cheers, leaving undisturbed a revolutionary gathering on the Nevsky Prospect."[5] The early troop defections served to encourage the demonstrators and enlarge the scale of the riots. In the meantime, a general strike amplified the unrest to critical proportions. The heavily charged atmosphere provided an irresistible opportunity for the many radicals who had "gone underground" to avoid detention by the czar's security police after the failed revolution of 1905.

THE EMERGENCE OF THE REVOLUTIONARY UNDERGROUND

The revolutionaries from 1905 had neither gone away nor accepted defeat, but had merely bided their time in exile, waiting for the next opportunity to rise. This was it. Resistance was not unified, but leading radicals were willing to ride the tide of popular revolt to overthrow the government. They could sort out leadership issues later. The more radical revolutionaries called on Nicholas to end the war. Even the czar's generals were losing confidence.

Nicholas heard the generals out as they advised him that his government could not survive, then announced his intention to abdicate, or step down from the throne, on March 2, 1917.

Historians generally agree that the czar was incompetent; he was certainly out of touch with the people, and he refused to share power with the Duma, but at the end he undoubtedly put his country before himself. Historian Richard Pipes, in *The Russian Revolution*, explains: "If Nicholas's foremost concern had been with preserving his throne he would have quickly made peace with Germany and used front-line troops to crush the rebellion in Petrograd and Moscow. He chose instead, to give up the crown to save the front."[6] With the dismantling of the monarchy, a new government was needed to take charge as quickly as possible. The end of the monarchy left a leadership vacuum, and principal players of the various factions rushed to fill it, not only the radical revolutionaries, but also the party favoring liberal democracy, called the Kadets, as well as the remaining monarchists.

THE PROVISIONAL GOVERNMENT

During Russia's previous uprisings, regional councils—or soviets—had been formed to provide local governance and rudimentary representation of workers and peasants. It was from these soviets that the leaders of the riots and strikes that started the revolution emerged.

Some members of the Duma, dissolved by the czar before his abdication, met on

Rasputin

One of the members of the czar's household was an unsavory madman named Rasputin, who became an influential adviser to Nicholas's wife, the czarina Alexandra, during the times she oversaw the government while the czar was at the front with his troops. Fearing disaster, a group of noblemen decided to murder Rasputin. Biographer Robert Massie describes the amateurish assassination in Nicholas and Alexandra.

"Alone in the cellar with his victim, [Prince] Yussoupov nervously offered Rasputin . . . poisoned cakes. Rasputin refused. Then, changing his mind, he gobbled two. Yussoupov watched, expecting to see him crumple in agony, but nothing happened. Then Rasputin asked for the [wine], which had also been poisoned. He swallowed two glasses, still with no effect. . . . In desperation [Yussoupov] rushed upstairs [to ask his co-conspirators] what he should do. . . . Steeling himself, Yussoupov volunteered to return to the cellar and complete the murder. Holding [a] Browning revolver behind his back, he went back down the stairs and found Rasputin seated, breathing heavily and calling for more wine. . . . Rasputin glared at the Prince [and] Yussoupov fired. . . . With a scream, Rasputin fell backward onto the white bearskin.

A moment later . . . Rasputin's face twitched and his left eye fluttered open. . . . Rasputin, foaming at the mouth, leaped to his feet, grabbed his murderer by the throat and tore an epaulet off his shoulder. [Rasputin then fled the house and was shot repeatedly.] When at last the body lay still in the crimson snow, it was rolled up in a blue curtain, bound with a rope and taken to a hole in the frozen Neva, where [it was pushed] through a hole in the ice. Three days later, when the body was found, the lungs were filled with water. Gregory Rasputin, his bloodstream filled with poison, his body punctured by bullets, had died by drowning."

Russian mystic and court favorite, Rasputin left his family and devoted himself to religion.

Aleksandr Kerensky, leader of the Provisional Government.

the new government. The Socialist radicals were wary about participating in the Provisional Government because to do so would signal their support for a government they considered not much better than the monarchy. The most active of the radicals were the Bolsheviks, a faction that broke away from the Russian Social Democratic Labor Party because they thought the party was not sufficiently radical. The non-Bolshevik Socialists did sponsor one important member of the new government: Aleksandr Kerensky, a moderate Socialist former member of the Duma accepted the post of minister of justice. The first head of the new government was Prince G. E. Lvov.

The real leader of the Provisional Government, however, was Kerensky, not Lvov. A man of indeterminate ideology, Kerensky had joined the radical Socialist Revolutionary Party as a young man. In the early days of the revolution, this party was just as important as the Bolsheviks, and Kerensky saw himself as a bridge between the radicals and the moderates. No revolutionary leader could maintain such a position, however, and indeed, radicals and moderates were at each other's throats from the beginning despite their common goal of replacing the monarchy.

Historians have not regarded Kerensky highly as a leader, but historian Richard Pipes sees his early popularity as a response to his emotional speeches, which could arouse a crowd. Pipes describes a speech Kerensky made to the Soviet of Workers and Soldiers' Deputies when he was seeking the position of minister of justice in the new Provisional

their own and formed a temporary executive committee in preparation for establishing the Provisional Government to replace the monarchy. They were joined by a committee from the Soviet of Workers and Soldiers' Deputies, which was active in the revolution of 1905, dormant since its failure, and now suddenly rejuvenated. Committee members from the Soviet were divided over participation in

Government: "He pledged that as a minister he would never betray democratic ideals. 'I cannot live without the people,' he shouted in his pathetic manner, 'and the moment you come to doubt me, kill me!' Having uttered these words, he made ready to faint. It was pure melodrama, but it worked."[7]

The Provisional Government was hampered from the beginning by interference from the soviets through their executive committee, known as Ispolkom. Though the soviets publicly took a hands-off position regarding central government affairs, they created both confusion and mischief as the "unofficial" watchdog of government activities.

For example, an early decree of the new government, known as "Order Number One," was issued in March at the insistence of Ispolkom. It democratized the military by ordering the election of representatives to the Soviet of Workers and Soldiers' Deputies and by abolishing many rank distinctions. Also in March, the strikes ended and those who had been arrested under czarist rule were granted amnesty. Revolutionary leaders who had fled the country could now return.

AN EXILE'S RETURN

Among the exiled radicals who reappeared on the scene of revolution was Vladimir Ilich Ulyanov, known as Lenin, who had been in Switzerland at the outbreak of the 1917 revolution. Long a prominent and vocal Socialist leader, Lenin arrived in Petrograd on April 3.

A brilliant revolutionary theoretician and strategist, Lenin lost no time in reestablishing his authority among the hard-core radicals, the Bolshevik faction of the Russian Social Democratic Labor Party. Shortly after his return, he made a speech to a group of Bolshevik leaders, in which he reiterated his plan for winning the revolution. This speech has become known as his "April Theses."

Lenin, Russian Communist and leader of the Bolsheviks.

LENIN'S "APRIL THESES" MANIFESTO

The April Theses summarized Lenin's plan to seize control of the revolution and place the Bolsheviks in power. He knew that these goals could not be realized under the Provisional Government as then constituted. This body, headed by a nobleman, Prince Lvov, and a middle-class Russian politician, Kerensky, would not advance the radical program of the Bolsheviks, or indeed allow Lenin himself much influence.

Therefore, rather than supporting the Provisional Government, and thus ensuring its survival, Lenin called for the Bolsheviks to withdraw their support. This move, he hoped, would cause the Lvov-Kerensky government to fail, opening an opportunity for the Bolsheviks to dominate its successor.

Another provision of Lenin's manifesto called for Russia's withdrawal from World War I. The war effort was eating up supplies and diverting peasants from their fields to fight at the front. Lenin's call to withdraw from the war increased his popularity, and thus support for the Bolsheviks, throughout the country.

Some of the provisions of Lenin's theses were quite unrealistic; for example, he wanted to abolish the police, the army, and the traditional government bureaucracy. However, two provisions that ultimately formed the foundation of the Bolshevik takeover and the formation of the Soviet Union were Lenin's call for nationalization of land and the creation of a republic of soviets; that is, governance by representatives of local councils to a central authority.

The Bolshevik Central Committee passed a negative resolution on the theses, and provincial Bolshevik committees condemned it. Nevertheless, Lenin's leadership position was so secure that the theses became the official Bolshevik position.

Meanwhile, another major figure in the revolution was preparing to return to Russia.

ANOTHER EXILE RETURNS

In early May 1917 another revolutionary leader ended his years of exile. Leon D. Trotsky, leader of the moderate Menshevik faction of the Russian Social Democratic Labor Party, returned to Russia from New York. At the beginning of the revolution, Trotsky was as influential in the party as Lenin. Trotsky, a militant Marxist who organized the Red Army, was nevertheless considered a moderate because he advocated a more gradual path to socialism than did Lenin and his Bolsheviks. Trotsky's ability to get along with Lenin was an important factor in the eventual Bolshevik triumph. At crucial moments when unity was essential for victory, Trotsky the moderate was able to convince his fellow Mensheviks to put aside their ideological differences with the Bolsheviks and support Lenin.

From a purely practical standpoint the main difference between the moderate Trotsky and the radical Lenin was Trotsky's willingness to cooperate with the Provisional Government. Thus it was not

Leon D. Trotsky organized the Red Army.

altogether surprising that, in the end, the two leaders would act in concert.

A Governing Coalition Is Formed

Most of the revolutionary activity in the first months of 1917 was centered in Petrograd and Moscow. By May 1917, however, anarchy, or lawlessness, had spread throughout the country.

In May the revolutionary factions came together to form a coalition, led by Kerensky, then minister of war. Its main purpose was to re-form the military and regain control of Russia's war effort.

Kerensky toured the war front, trying to appeal to the soldiers' sense of patriotism. Thanks largely to "Order Number One," as well as the general chaos gripping the country, however, the breakdown in discipline was too far advanced to respond to Kerensky's emotional appeals, and anarchy spread.

By the middle of June, Lenin and Trotsky had formed an alliance of Bolsheviks and Mensheviks, which strengthened the influence of the Bolsheviks as well as their drive for a Socialist takeover of the revolution.

June drew to a close. Russian troops defeated the Austrians at Lwow, capital of Galicia, taking tens of thousands of prisoners. However, this victory soon turned sour when German troops rushed to the rescue of the Austrians. The undisciplined, ill-provisioned, hungry Russian soldiers were routed, and the disgrace contributed to further unrest throughout Russia, in what became known as the "July Days."

Kerensky (center) at the war front encouraging his troops.

THE "JULY DAYS"

The disastrous retreat from the advancing German army at Lwow had a galvanizing effect on the July unrest, and the breakdown in law and order reached a dangerous level. On July 3 antigovernment rioting broke out in Petrograd.

Kerensky, about to be named prime minister of the Provisional Government, believed that the Germans had known in advance that there would be rioting in the capital and that Lenin and other Bolsheviks were responsible both for orchestrating the riots and for informing the Germans. In retaliation, Kerensky ordered the arrest of Bolsheviks and the closing of Bolshevik newspaper offices. Lenin went into hiding in Finland, and other Bolshevik leaders took similar measures to protect themselves.

The July Days uprisings had created major dissensions among the factions attempting to influence the outcome of the revolution. Lenin, especially, felt the time had come to break away from the non-Bolshevist factions. At the Bolshevik party congress late in July, Lenin sent word from Finland that the time for cooperation with all the other participants in the revolution was over. The Bolsheviks would go their own way.

THE BOLSHEVIKS PREPARE TO SEIZE POWER

The Bolsheviks' projected power grab began to look feasible as Kerensky's Provisional Government increasingly lost the confidence of the soldiers and workers. Nevertheless, Bolshevik resolve wavered.

A NEW ORDER IN THE FACTORIES

At the outbreak of the revolution of 1917, employee committees, established as a result of the 1905 revolution, assumed many management functions in Petrograd factories. This movement bolstered Socialist influence in the revolution. David Mandel, in The Petrograd Workers and the Fall of the Old Regime, *describes the function of these committees.*

"The demand for elected representatives in the factory had a long history, and, in fact, several large factories already had semi-legal 'councils of elders' before the revolution. These served to represent the workers before the administration. The March 10 [1917] agreement between the Soviet [of Soldiers and Workers' Deputies] and the [factory] owners legalised these committees, providing for their election in all industrial enterprises. . . . Virtually everywhere they raised the demand for 'control over internal order. . . . [This] represented the essence of the workers' conception of the new order in the factories."

After encouraging the July riots, many radicalized troops were ready to move against the government on July 3, but members of the Bolshevik Central Committee urged them to return to their barracks. Emboldened by the troops' showing, the committee then adopted a resolution calling for the overthrow of the Provisional Government by force. Many disaffected moderates transferred their support to the Bolsheviks.

During all the confusion in the short time between the February bread riots and the July Days, the Bolshevik Party, as well as its military arm, the Red Guards, had been growing in numerical strength. In May the party had some eighty thousand members; by August membership had grown to more than two hundred thousand. That may seem to be a very small number in a country of many millions, but not in comparison with other revolutionary factions. The Bolsheviks were becoming a formidable political force, and an important factor in their strength was the growing support of the peasants throughout the country.

The peasants did not support Lenin because of his communist philosophy; few even knew what that philosophy was. They believed, however, that the Bolsheviks favored taking land from the powerful landowners and giving it to the peasants who had worked on the big estates for so many generations. They could not foresee that in a short time the land would be taken back by the same Bolsheviks in the name of "collectivization." For the time being, the peasants were on Lenin's side. Their support in turn allowed Lenin to reject compromise.

The Bolsheviks had used the months since the February insurrection to rally the support necessary not only to seize power but to hold it. At last, with growing support, the Bolsheviks were ready to make a move.

THE OCTOBER REVOLUTION

The Bolsheviks' final victory was surprisingly easy. The initial stages of the October Revolution were set in motion by Trotsky, because Lenin was still in hiding, fearing a repeat of the July Days crackdown on opponents of the Provisional Government. Trotsky was on the scene as head of the Military Revolutionary Committee as well as head of the powerful Petrograd Soviet. In the chaotic atmosphere of February to October 1917, a staggering number of councils, committees, conferences, factions, coalitions, and other governing bodies struggled for a toehold of power, some with a life span of days.

Richard Pipes believes the coup d'etat occurred in two stages: first the April and July events, and then, in October, the final coup. In the first stage, he writes, "Lenin attempted to take power in Petrograd by means of street demonstrations backed by armed force." The second stage was orchestrated by Trotsky because Lenin was still in Finland. Trotsky "disguised preparation for a Bolshevik takeover behind the facade of a [phony and unauthorized] Congress of Soviets, while relying on special shock troops to seize the nerve centers of the government."[8]

An Anarchist's Disillusionment

Emma Goldman, a Russian-born American anarchist who was deported back to Russia in 1919, gives her unflattering impressions of life after the revolution in My Disillusionment in Russia.

"Though widely differing in their political views, nearly all of my callers related an identical story, the story of the high tide of the Revolution, of the wonderful spirit that led the people forward, of the possibilities of the masses, the role of the Bolsheviki as the spokesmen of the most extreme revolutionary slogans and their betrayal of the Revolution after they had secured power. . . . They supported their statements by [much] evidence. . . . They told of the persecution of their comrades, the shooting of innocent men and women, the criminal inefficiency, waste, and destruction. . . .

Most of [the Bolshevik's governing] methods spring from their lack of understanding of the character and the needs of the Russian people and the mad obsession of dictatorship, which is not even the dictatorship of the proletariat but the dictatorship of a small group over the proletariat.

When I broached the subject of the People's Soviets and the elections my visitors smiled. 'Elections! There are no such things in Russia, unless you call threats and terrorism elections. It is by these alone that the Bolsheviki secure a majority. A few Mensheviki, Social Revolutionists, or Anarchists are permitted to slip into the Soviets, but they have not the shadow of a chance to be heard.'"

Emma Goldman, a devout anarchist, spent a long career pleading unpopular cases.

Lenin emerged from hiding on October 24 and assumed command of the overthrow of the Provisional Government. That night, Bolshevik insurgents took control of bridges, railways, and the telephone exchange. Kerensky, at the Winter Palace, concluded that his Provisional Government was falling and made preparations to flee not only the palace, but the country. He remained at the head of the Provisional Government until its collapse, but would eventually flee to New York, where he led a quiet middle-class life until his death in 1970.

Other members of the Provisional Government were arrested. The October Revolution, and indeed the Russian Revolution, had fallen decisively to the Bolsheviks, and in particular to Lenin. As historian Robert Daniels puts it, "Like the displacement of the tsar by the Provisional Government, the transfer of power to the soviets was quickly accepted almost everywhere in the country, with relatively little violence."[9]

The struggle for power had not ended, though, for the Bolsheviks had yet to consolidate their power. Sadly for the Russian people, a bloody civil war would be fought before Lenin gained firm control of the country.

2 The Lenin Era: 1917–1924

There is no question that Lenin, leader of the Bolsheviks, won the revolution. His successful tactics included unilaterally dissolving a representative assembly, making false promises, and simply outlasting his opponents. He promised democracy and delivered totalitarianism and repression. He promised land redistribution for the peasants and delivered state-run collective farms. He promised independence for non-Russian regions conquered by the Russian empire and delivered so-called Soviet republics. He set the tone for all future Communist rule.

Historian Ian Grey describes Lenin's immediate goal on seizing power:

> In *The State and Revolution* Lenin set out concisely the steps to be taken to overthrow capitalist society and to create the new order. . . . He knew that he must at once secure the position of the party by gaining stronger popular support for it especially among the peasant masses.[10]

To succeed, Lenin would have to appear to be carrying out his promises of land and peace. He had no intention of enacting real

Setting the tone for all future Communist rule, Lenin won the revolution.

Hungry peasants search for food in the city dump after the revolution.

land reform, however, and tried to convince peasants that collectivization, his real goal, was tantamount to redistribution. It would not work.

Meanwhile, before promises to the masses could be addressed, Lenin intended to reinforce his party's control of the country. The October Revolution was not the end of the Bolshevik struggle for power.

THE BOLSHEVIKS TAKE OVER

The October Revolution, which confirmed Bolshevik rule, was a power grab, or coup d'etat, rather than a real revolution. The czar was deposed, and the Provisional Government that had attempted to take his place was generally accepted by the people. The Bolsheviks had then ousted the leaders of this government and seized control of the central bureaucracy in Petrograd. Although officials of the Provisional Government had been removed by force, the Bolsheviks had not won a military victory and still lacked broad popular support.

In the wake of the Bolshevik victory, and still in the midst of World War I, Russia was in shambles. The country's infant industrial base was insufficient to supply both the military and civilian sectors while the war raged. Furthermore, industrialization had not reached the agricultural sector, and peasant masses could not serve both agriculture and the military, and so both suffered.

Russia's people were largely illiterate and for the most part desperately poor. An infrastructure of roads, bridges, railroads, and utilities was almost nonexistent. Thus on the eve of the meeting of the All-Russian Congress of Soviets in late October 1917, the Bolsheviks faced grave challenges.

LENIN FORMS A GOVERNMENT

The October Congress, a gathering of Soviet representatives that had supported or participated in the revolution, confirmed majority control by the Bolsheviks. Lenin took this vote as the basis for the legitimacy of his leadership, and he set about forming a governing cabinet, which would be called the

Joseph Dzhugashvili, also known as Joseph Stalin.

Council of People's Commissars. Commissars are similar to cabinet secretaries or government ministers in Western governments. Lenin's fifteen-member cabinet would be composed only of Bolsheviks, including Lenin himself as president of the council, and Leon Trotsky as commissar of foreign affairs. Further down the list in importance, "a little-known professional revolutionary from Georgia, Joseph Dzhugashvili, alias Stalin, the Man of Steel was made commissar for nationalities,"[11] according to Robert Daniels. The commissars were at the top of the government bureaucracies.

During the czar's reign, Lenin had denounced and promised to eliminate the bureaucracy that administered the day-to-day operations of the government. One of the many ironies of Soviet history is that on taking the reins of the new Bolshevik government, Lenin found that he needed an even larger bureaucracy to achieve centralized control. Those who expected local soviets to be self-governing according to Marxist theory were to be disappointed. Lenin was quick to rationalize the centralization of power: Without the protection of the central Bolshevik government, he said, workers at the local level would continue to be vulnerable to exploitation, and, anyway, self-government would come later. Lenin spoke of democracy, but he made it clear that the country was to have a strong central government.

An example of Lenin's approach to governing occurred shortly after he took power and set the stage for the coming totalitarian terror. Before the October Revolution, Lenin had demanded that the Provisional Government convene representatives of all political parties. Kerensky scheduled this so-called Constituent Assembly for November. After the October Congress confirmed Lenin's leadership, he wanted to postpone the assembly indefinitely, but Trotsky talked him into letting it meet as scheduled.

Daniel Diller writes that "the Bolshevik party . . . won only 170 out of 707 seats in the assembly. . . . The Constituent Assembly met for the first time on January 18, 1918, and immediately challenged Bolshevik policies."[12] The following day, Lenin declared the assembly closed and sent troops into the hall to make sure everybody went home. Henceforth, no deviation would be tolerated. Lenin's intentions were now clear: All pretense that the government of Russia would have democratic features had been abandoned.

The ruling Bolshevik Party was to be like a pyramid; at the bottom, rank-and-file party members would select delegates to the party congress, which would in turn choose the Central Committee, which would elect the Politburo. The Politburo was made up of the ministers who directed the bureaucracy and selected the party chairman. Lenin had founded the Party and had always been its chairman. There was no set term of office; Lenin held the position as long as he lived. Party congresses were in session only periodically, to approve an agenda for the government now centered in the new capital, Moscow. Because, however, the agenda, as well as nominations to the Politburo and the Central Committee, was dictated by Lenin, the only role of the congress was to rubber-stamp Lenin's choices.

Peasants buy and trade goods in a Russian market.

Although Lenin's political philosophy was derived from the theories of Karl Marx, who preached that revolution would, by stages, lead to pure communism, he was prepared to make important deviations. Nevertheless, he wasted no time in changing the name of the Bolshevik Party to the Communist Party, a signal that his would be a Marxist government.

THE ROCKY ROAD TO SOCIALISM: INDUSTRY AND AGRICULTURE

The massive task of nationalizing Russian industry clearly could not be accomplished overnight. Thus Lenin proceeded by stages along the road to socialism. In the transfer from private to government ownership, Lenin took some steps toward egalitarianism, paying lip service to social and economic equality. For example, one of his proclamations abolished all titles and legal class divisions. This move was also aimed at increasing production, a goal that was not fully achieved. The workers were exhausted both by the hardships of World War I and by the year-long internal power struggle.

The peasants, still the backbone of Russian agriculture, were exhausted, too, and Lenin realized the need to give them hope for a better future. Thus he once more promised land to the peasants and allowed them some freedom to trade their produce. These decisions were contradictions of communist philosophy. But Lenin was always a pragmatist: Nationalization of industry and agriculture was not leading grateful workers and peasants to cooperate and support the new government, so Lenin backtracked, postponing complete collectivization. No such retreat from communist principles was required, however, to achieve another Bolshevik goal: reorganizing the army.

REORGANIZING THE ARMY AND SHAPING THE SOVIETS

To gain control of the army, Lenin succeeded where Kerensky failed: He appealed to the class consciousness of ordinary soldiers, who were disheartened and ready for change after the disap-

pointing showing against the Germans. Many officers supported the new Bolshevik government simply because it was the government, and thus appeared to offer the most obvious route to continue their careers.

In January 1918, Lenin reorganized the army along Socialist principles and renamed it the Red Army. Richard Pipes explains that

> Even after taking power, the Bolsheviks continued to dismantle what was left of the old army, depriving the officers of the little authority they still retained. Initially, they ordered that officers be elected, and then abolished military ranks, vesting the power to make command appointments in soldiers' soviets.[13]

This arrangement was somewhat reminiscent of Order Number One, allowing soldiers to elect their superior officers, and it was unworkable because it contradicted basic military discipline. Like Lenin's promise to withdraw from World War I, this decree was made to gain the support of the lower ranks of the army.

Once Lenin had control of the army, he turned his attention to the local soviets across the country. Imposing strict Party discipline on these diverse assemblies was harder. Daniel Diller outlines Lenin's approach: "Since the Bolsheviks were not well represented in many city and rural soviets, [Lenin's agents] resorted to tactics ranging from political campaigning to intimidation and the use of armed force."[14] By the end of 1918, the new Bolshevik government was firmly in control of most of the country, in part due to Lenin's terror tactics, which remain frightening examples of state ruthlessness.

THE RED TERROR

Once in power, Lenin moved swiftly to consolidate his authority. His strategy was to enforce a policy of zero toleration for deviation from his command. One of his first actions was the formation of the Cheka, a secret police organization that would search out and kill those Lenin regarded as "enemies of the state." In addition to their assigned executions, Cheka agents frequently shot innocent people to heighten the atmosphere of terror. Richard Pipes quotes Lenin's own rationalization for what became known as the Red Terror: "'What is better—to put in prison a few dozen or a few hundred inciters, *guilty or not*, conscious or not, or to lose thousands of Red Army soldiers and workers? The former is better.'"[15] Lenin's logic was that creating an atmosphere of terror would prevent antigovernment protest. Moreover, to that same end, Lenin had no qualms about making promises he did not intend to fulfill.

Before coming to power Lenin had made many fine promises to gain support for a Bolshevik takeover of the government. In addition to land reform, he had guaranteed freedom of the press, toleration of opposition political parties, and self-determination for the non-Russian republics that were subjects of the Russian empire, such as Ukraine. All of these promises were broken. Although by 1920 Ukraine, Belorussia, Armenia, Azerbaijan, and Georgia were called "Soviet Socialist Republics," they were not sovereign republics with control over their own affairs. Indeed, as the central government grew over time, these second-class states lost even more autonomy. Not only did Lenin betray these so-called republics, he began taking away what little freedom Soviet citizens had.

TIGHT CONTROL OF RUSSIAN SOCIETY

The Red Terror was more than just persecution of the enemies of the new Communist government. It involved the transformation of society. Though the czarist government had been totalitarian, it had unofficially tolerated some activities of some labor unions, soviets, and the very revolutionary parties, such as the Bolsheviks, that overthrew the czar. Lenin did not make that mistake. No one who threatened state security (as Lenin had, in fomenting revolution) was allowed to leave the country (as Lenin had done repeatedly when his anticzarist activities attracted unwanted attention). Under the new Communist regime, dissidents were arrested, and those deemed dangerous counterrevolutionaries were executed. Lenin's repressions under the Red Terror, in addition to random arrests, included the suppression of free speech and labor unions and encouragement of informers.

Indeed, Lenin went so far as to abolish the law itself and replace the rule of law with something he called "revolutionary conscience." According to Pipes, the authorities would "dispose of anyone they

disliked and legitimized pogroms [organized persecution] against their opponents," on the grounds of fulfilling "revolutionary conscience."[16]

Yet despite all the broken promises that preceded Lenin's Red Terror, there was one promise he intended to keep: withdrawal from World War I.

RUSSIA WITHDRAWS FROM WORLD WAR I

To extract itself from the war, Russia signed a humiliating treaty with Germany, negotiated at Brest Litovsk in Poland on March 3, 1918. The treaty was opposed by most within the Bolshevist inner circle, but Lenin, the realist, wanted it,

and he prevailed. Robert Daniels explains: "Russia had to concede German control of occupied Poland and of the Baltic provinces. . . . This was the worst territorial setback suffered by Russia in almost four centuries."[17] Nevertheless, withdrawal allowed Lenin to concentrate on defeating the growing number of dissidents opposing Bolshevik rule. This dissent, fueled by the withdrawal from the war, was sufficiently powerful to result in a bloody civil war.

CIVIL WAR

The civil war was to some extent a counterrevolution. Though the Bolsheviks were now in control of the country, many Russians who had supported the revolution—meaning the revolution of 1917 that had installed the Provisional Government—strongly opposed Bolshevik rule and especially resented Lenin's withdrawal from World War I. These dissidents, known as the Whites, attracted aid from the remaining Allies, especially Britain and the United States.

When World War I ended with the Treaty of Versailles in 1919, however, Allied interest in supporting the Whites in the civil war waned, and the fortunes of the Reds revived. The civil war subsided in European Russia by early 1920, the year of the end of American postwar occupation.

Lenin was at last free to build his new state, the Union of Soviet Socialist Republics (USSR), or more simply, the Soviet Union. By 1929 the "republics" included Turkmen, Uzbek, Tajjik, as well as Ukraine and others incorporated earlier. But to finish his task of creating a Socialist state, Lenin would need to supplement his terror tactics.

Whereas Lenin had used the Red Terror to eliminate opposition to the new government and to his own authority, he would develop what he called "war communism" to quickly convert Russian society to a system run on Communist economic and political principles.

WAR COMMUNISM

"War communism" was a slogan collectively referring to the measures Lenin intended to take in order to transform traditional Russian society to a Communist

Cheka agents frequently shot innocent people to heighten the atmosphere of terror during Lenin's Red Terror.

THE KRONSTADT REBELLION

A rebellion at the Kronstadt naval base in 1921 might have convinced Lenin that War Communism should be abandoned. Sailors at the base, suffering from the famine created by the drought and by war communism, presented a resolution demanding that the new government keep its promises to return power and self-determination to the people. The government ministers knew that to stay in power, they would have to crush the rebellion. This they achieved by slaughtering tens of thousands of the Kronstadt sailors. Biographer Robert Payne sums up the episode in The Life and Death of Lenin.

"The sailors of Kronstadt were brave men, but inept revolutionaries. They believed wholeheartedly in their pacific propaganda. It was as though they suffered from some strange disease compounded of hope and benevolence, and believed they could infect the whole of Russia with their disease. It never occurred to them until too late that Lenin was implacable and ruthless, and would sign the death warrant of the Kronstadt sailors with the same careless ease as he had signed the death warrant of the bourgeoisie."

economic system in a very short time. To that end, Lenin believed he first had to abolish private property and free markets for the exchange of goods. The government took over all banks and industry. All agricultural workers, factory workers, and other jobholders now worked for the government.

Since all produce now belonged to the government, which had taken over much of the land in the name of collectivization, agents were authorized to requisition the harvest and to pay the peasants a meager wage. In protest, peasants produced less and hid whatever they could. The subsequent pattern of cutbacks and hoardings, along with a prolonged drought, resulted in severe food shortages that killed as many as 5 million people in the early 1920s. War communism clearly did not work.

War communism did immense harm by disrupting the established trading system and discouraging agricultural production. The flawed system, however, saved many from starvation essentially because the abrupt abolition of the normal ways of doing business forced creation of an alternative economy. The brutal goverment takeover of production inspired an underground trading system, or black market, in operation to the present day. Richard Pipes confirms that those charged with implementing war communism realized the role of the black market: "Strict enforcement [of war communism], even if it were possible, would bring about economic catastrophe: Communist sources conceded that without the illicit trade in food, which supplied the urban population with two-thirds of its bread, the cities would have starved."[18]

Lenin would have to find a new strategy to impose communism on the USSR. He turned next to the so-called New Economic Policy.

THE NEW ECONOMIC POLICY

In 1921 Lenin's plan for reversing the economic collapse created by war communism was to reinstate a limited form of capitalism, which he called the New Economic Policy (NEP). He regarded this retreat from socialism as temporary. Robert Payne explains:

> The New Economic Policy involved a radical departure from the theory of communism as Lenin described it. . . . Lenin knew that he was opening the way to a modified form of capitalism. . . . The peasants were allowed to trade their surplus grain on the open market. The idea of selling for profit, which had previously been regarded as a crime against the state, was now officially encouraged.[19]

Economic collapse was not the only cause of famine in 1921, however. Drought, dust storms, and invasions of locusts forced many peasants to abandon their farms and seek refuge in the towns, which could neither feed them nor shelter them without aid from abroad.

A future U.S. president, Herbert Hoover, then head of the American Relief Administration, was permitted by Lenin to organize distributions of food to the starving people, enlisting Russian workers in the effort. According to Payne, "About half of the Russians who served under the Americans in the relief organizations were later arrested on the grounds that contact with the Americans must inevitably have led them to become 'counterrevolutionary elements.'"[20] U.S. aid was desperately needed and saved many from starvation, but it was the NEP that reversed the economic decline.

Disappointing as it was for Lenin to have to keep postponing complete collectivization, the New Economic Policy worked very well. Diller's evaluation is that "the NEP succeeded in stabilizing the country and revitalizing the economy. By 1928 production in most industries had recovered to pre–World War I levels. This revitalization was accompanied by an increase in prosperous peasants and small business owners."[21] The NEP was one of the few positive successes in Lenin's short tenure as leader of the Soviet Union.

LENIN'S LEGACY

Most of Lenin's energies as a revolutionary were spent acquiring and keeping power. A politician both pragmatic and opportunistic, he was willing to forgo principle on the road to a Communist society. Ironically, Lenin's periodic retreats from classical Marxism preserved his leadership and kept the Communists in power.

The NEP, a retreat from collectivization, was an example of Lenin's pragmatism.

LENIN JUSTIFIES PEACE WITH GERMANY

Lenin's proposal to pull out of World War I and make a separate peace with Germany was bitterly opposed by most Bolshevik leaders. They believed that communism in Russia could survive only if world revolution broke out in Western Europe, and they feared that peace with capitalist Germany would jeopardize the revolution. Richard Pipes, in The Russian Revolution, *presents Lenin's views on this issue:*

"Lenin was prepared to make peace with the Central Powers [Germany] on any terms as long as they left him a power base. The resistance which he encountered in party ranks grew out of the belief (which he shared) that the Bolshevik government could survive only if a revolution broke out in Western Europe and the conviction (which he did not fully share) that this was bound to happen at any moment."

Lenin's primary concern was for the immediate survival of his government. Lenin argued that "Our tactics ought to rest . . . [on the principle of] how to ensure more reliably and hopefully for the socialist revolution the possibility of consolidating itself or even surviving *in one country* until such time as other countries join in."

So was his ruthless treatment of the non-Russian republics in the Soviet Union, such as Ukraine. Before he came to power, he had referred to them as oppressed colonies of the Russian empire and promised them self-determination. Once in power, he brutally put down all efforts by the republics to leave the union.

In the process of establishing the first Marxist state, Lenin developed a tyrannical model of government that subsequent Soviet rulers would follow. It is possible that no leader dedicated to maintaining civil and economic liberties in Russia during the early years of the revolution would have survived challenges by rivals willing to sacrifice popular rights for the sake of quick results. It

is certain that Lenin took no chances in this respect.

Instead of granting the people the rights he had once promised, he surrounded himself with deputies willing to conspire and commit atrocities to control the population—always insisting that his goal was the greatest good for the greatest number and that the end justified the means.

LENIN'S FINAL YEARS

Beginning in May 1922 Lenin suffered a series of strokes. He recovered from the first sufficiently to resume his duties, but in March 1923 a final stroke left him per-

Stalin (right) took advantage of Lenin's poor health by positioning himself to take control.

meetings and rallies, allowing opportunistic deputies, especially Joseph Stalin, time to position themselves for the power struggle sure to follow his death. Roy A. Medvedev, the distinguished Soviet historian, describes Stalin's cunning manipulation of Lenin during his last illness: "Stalin, with his characteristic callousness and meanness . . . tried to isolate Lenin, to deprive him of all information about current party business and disagreements, on the pretext of concern for Lenin's health."[22]

In a letter to colleagues in the Central Committee that did not surface publicly until after Lenin's death, the first Communist dictator asked the committee to fire Stalin. Stalin had previously elevated himself through the post created for him, that of general secretary of the Communist Party, to a level never intended by Lenin. Louis Aragon quotes Lenin's thoughts on the man who ultimately succeeded him:

manently weakened, and his physical state deteriorated markedly. Although he managed to maintain control of the government up to his death in 1924, his physical incapacity kept him away from

Lenin's tomb at the Red Square in Moscow.

Comrade Stalin, now that he has become secretary-general, has gathered to himself unlimited power, and I am not sure whether he may always use it with enough caution. . . . Stalin is too coarse, and although this fault is perfectly tolerable amongst us . . . this is no longer the case in one who carries out the functions of secretary-general.[23]

Lenin died on January 21, 1924, and his tomb became a secular shrine, attracting throngs of visitors daily for decades. The state also honored Lenin by renaming the former capital city Leningrad.

3 The Stalin Era: 1924–1953

Joseph Stalin was born in 1879 in Georgia, a mountainous region of Russia later reorganized as a Soviet republic. He was enrolled in a seminary at age fifteen but was expelled just before graduating. He then joined the Russian Social Democratic Labor Party, becoming one of its most radical advocates of revolution. When the party split in 1903, Stalin joined the more radical faction, the Bolsheviks. With Lenin's approval, in 1907 he helped finance Bolshevik activities by organizing the robbery of a carriage transporting a large sum of the czar's money. After the 1917 revolution he became one of Lenin's trusted lieutenants, rising steadily in influence.

The office of general secretary of the Communist Party had been created for Stalin in 1922 because Lenin regarded him as a loyal plodder well suited to the administrative duties he envisioned for the post. It was by no means meant to be a stepping-stone to higher authority; however, Stalin made it one. He used his new position as a platform for some entry-level networking, traveling around the Soviet Union to meet and cultivate minor provincial Party officials, who became his allies in his later climb to power.

POLITBURO POLITICS

The Politburo had given Lenin unified support in deference to his skills as a mediator and his long history as leader and founder of the Party. But although he partially recovered from the disabling stroke

Stalin (left) became one of Lenin's (center) most trusted lieutenants and rose steadily in influence.

he suffered in May 1922 and resumed much of his leadership role, the unity of the Politburo disintegrated. In this uncertain atmosphere, a governing troika, or three-person steering committee, consisting of Stalin, Lev B. Kamenev, and Grigorii V. Zinov'ev, emerged to oppose the leadership ambitions of Trotsky and of Nikolay I. Bukharin, one of whom many believed would be Lenin's heir. Lenin had seemed to derive his governing authority from ongoing consultation with other Party leaders that resulted in consensus. In truth, he dominated the Politburo through force of will and his demon-

Nikolay Bukharin advocated gradual transformation to communism by continuing with Lenin's New Economic Policy.

strated ruthlessness. Politburo support would not automatically be extended to the new leadership troika.

Stalin soon had to compete with the other two members of the troika as well as the other claimants to power, Trotsky and Bukharin. Kamenev and Zinov'ev formed an alliance with Trotsky against Stalin, but were stripped of their influence through Stalin's connections as Party secretary.

The emergence of three claimants to succession, presenting a facade of collective leadership, demonstrated one of the weaknesses of the government Lenin had established. Because power in the Soviet Union flowed from the top down, when the leader at the top died, a leadership vacuum followed. No democratic process existed for election of leaders by the people.

The struggle for power after Lenin's death was more than a contest to fill the top office of the still-young Soviet Union; it was also an ideological struggle among adherents of opposing ideas for achieving the ideal Communist state. Trotsky and his supporters, who were considered the left wing of the Party, advocated complete collectivization as soon as possible in Russia, coupled with an ambitious foreign policy that included active encouragement of worldwide revolution to ensure the success of communism. The right wing, represented by Bukharin and his allies, concentrated on domestic affairs, advocating gradual transformation to communism by continuing Lenin's New Economic Policy, which allowed small enterprises to operate privately while large industry was centralized.

COMMUNISM IN ONE COUNTRY

Stalin chose a position somewhere between the two extremes, adopting a theory once advanced by Lenin: "communism in one country." This doctrine called for aggressive development of socialism in the Soviet Union without the need for world revolution and regardless of whether other countries likewise adopted socialism. This position was closer to the beliefs of Bukharin, and Stalin gained the right-winger's support, which gave Stalin sufficient strength to remove Trotsky and his allies from their positions in the Party. Trotsky was discredited and forced into exile; his allies in the Party were persecuted and many were expelled. Roy Medvedev records that "hundreds of Trotskyites were arrested, some for a real but many for an imaginary connection with Trotsky."[24]

Not until the spring of 1929, however, did Stalin move against Bukharin and his associates, to stand alone as the undisputed leader of the Soviet Union.

In many respects "communism in one country" or "socialism in one country," as it was sometimes called, was simply Lenin's NEP under another name. In other respects it was a rhetorical device that allowed Stalin to manipulate economic affairs, advancing and retreating from the actual practice of communism while voicing strict adherence to Marxist principles. Though the era of NEP, which outlived Lenin by roughly four years, was a retreat from communism, it was by no means a retreat for the Communist Party. Stalin used these years to consolidate his own authority, establish relations with other European countries, and plan for transformation to "real" communism.

Stalin's chosen method to achieve communism was to adopt a rigid timetable for implementing the needed transformation to a controlled, centralized planning system. He set goals for achieving these changes in five-year increments and spelled out the details in a series of five-year plans. In the beginning, at least, Stalin seemed to be using the new system to further the NEP.

NEP UNDER STALIN

The NEP era allowed for a degree of freedom of expression that had not been tolerated under Lenin and would not return until the era of glasnost in the 1980s. As the authors of *Soviet Union: A Country Study* indicate, however, Stalin granted such freedoms only when he felt the state would benefit: "Communist writers Maksim Gorky and Vladimir Maiakovskii were active during this time, but other authors, many of whose works were later repressed, published work lacking socialist political content. Film, as a means of influencing a largely illiterate society, received encouragement from the state."[25] At the same time, schools were expanded. Night school for working adults addressed the pervasiveness of illiteracy and well-prepared members of the lower classes were provided with higher education.

These transitory freedoms were revoked whenever it suited Stalin's purpose.

The real purpose of authoritarian relaxation during NEP was to allow economic recovery from too rapid collectivization.

During this period social attitudes became more permissive; abortion was legalized and divorce was made more readily available. Traditional social institutions such as marriage were intentionally undermined to facilitate a shift of loyalties from family and the church to the state. Religious practice, in particular, was discouraged in accordance with Marx's belief that it served a counterrevolutionary purpose—namely, to dull the political sensibilities of the masses, who otherwise might fail to appreciate the wisdom of the Communist form of government. Thus atheism was promoted and churches were closed and, sometimes, torn down. The attempt to shift individual loyalties to the state also included encouraging people to inform the authorities about friends and family members not sufficiently dedicated to communism.

Although by 1925 NEP had raised agricultural production to pre–World War I levels, peasant farmers remained dissatisfied with commodity prices and further reduced production in protest. Increasing agricultural output led to a dilemma: Increasing industrialization was needed to supply technologically advanced farm machinery that would improve farm production, but industrialization could not proceed without factory workers, who could only be pulled from the agricultural sector. Thus neither agriculture nor industry flourished.

Stalin's plan of collectivization was to transform small and scattered peasant plots into large farms.

Stalin's solution to this dilemma was the First Five-Year Plan, announced in 1928. The plan was to rapidly bolster the industrial infrastructure by financing its development through state-owned, centrally planned, agricultural collectives. Millions of small, inefficient, ill-equipped peasant farms would be combined into large, well-run collectives. Stalin expressed his faith in collectivization in his *Collected Works:* "The solution lies in the transformation of small and scattered peasants' plots into large consolidated farms based on the joint cultivation of land using new superior techniques."[26] This brief definition, however, failed to provide a workable plan for achieving the massive changes represented by collectivization.

Peasants who refused to cooperate in collectivization were shot or exiled to the harsh regions of Siberia.

COLLECTIVIZATION

Collectivization was very unpopular among the peasants subject to the process, especially the kulaks, who were quite well off, and in some cases rich. NEP had benefited the kulaks, allowing them to increase their acreage and livestock, and collectivization required them to give up their gains. In December 1929 Stalin announced a policy to eliminate the kulak class.

Stalin ordered army units into the countryside to implement collectivization, and peasants who refused to cooperate were punished according to the level of their opposition. The most vigorous protesters were shot. Others were exiled to the harsh eastern region of Siberia; still others were sent to labor camps and their property turned over to government managers. Ian Grey estimates that "more than five million kulaks were deported to Siberia and the arctic north, and of them at least a quarter perished. Many more were killed in their villages and in trying to defend their property."[27] By 1932, toward the completion of the First Five-Year Plan, more than 60 percent of the countryside had been collectivized. The total would eventually rise to 90 percent.

But collectivization was not a success. The peasants resisted by butchering and eating their livestock, destroying their implements, burning their crops, and otherwise preventing the government from profiting from their work. As a result, in

A Stalinist Education

Writer Richard Lourie, in his book Russia: An Oral History From the Revolution to the Present, *records the story of a Soviet man reminiscing about his school experience during the Stalin era.*

"Our teacher was a real Stalinist. Cruel, tough as nails, she ruled with an iron hand. But she was always emphasizing that we were all brothers, all equal. All problems could be solved through her. We were supposed to go to her and squeal on our classmates—Petrov copied his homework from so and so. She encouraged us to inform on each other. In the classroom there was a large portrait of Pavlik Morozov. We were told that during collectivization some of the peasants hid their grain. Pavlik's father hid his grain too and Pavlik informed on him. He was a hero, a real Pioneer [boy scout], who had helped his country. He did not spare his own father for the good of the country. A Pioneer is supposed to tell the truth and that's what Pavlik did. And it was for telling the truth that he was killed by some of the other peasants. The country and the party are more important than your father, that was the conclusion we were supposed to reach."

Education during the Stalin era was strict and tough. Children were encouraged to inform on each other and on their own families.

Stalin became obsessed with achieving rapid industrialization and stressed the manufacturing of farm implements, automobiles, machine tools, and electric power plants.

the mid-1930s a famine engulfed a large part of the country, especially Ukraine and the northern Caucasus, and an estimated 5 to 10 million people died of starvation.

STATE INDUSTRIALIZATION: THE FIVE-YEAR PLANS

The other side of the First Five-Year Plan, and two subsequent plans, was industrialization. Perhaps because the country had suffered so greatly during World War I, when its industrial base was inadequate to supply the needs of the army, Stalin became obsessed with achieving rapid industrialization. He formed a state planning commission, called Gosplan, under his (and other high officials') direct supervision.

Because the Soviet Union lagged so far behind other industrialized countries, the most important industrial program was geared toward producing machine tools, that is, building machines that build other machines. Stalin also emphasized manufacturing farm implements, automobiles, and electric power plants.

In their push to catch up with the industrialized nations of the West, however, the planners neglected many needs of the Soviet people. Food was scarce, sanitation and water quality poor, and housing inadequate, especially in the cities. Conditions did not improve as the First Five-Year Plan was succeeded by the Second and Third, which focused on refining the First by improving the quality of output while still concentrating on heavy industry.

A NEW SOVIET ELITE EMERGES

Collectivization in the countryside and industrialization in the cities deprived Soviet citizens of basic freedoms such as the ability to choose where to live and what jobs to take. Movement within the country was restricted by a system of internal passports, making it difficult for people dissatisfied with working or living conditions in one area to move to another. At the same time, Stalin violated Lenin's most precious commitment to Marxism: the equality of all citizens. Stalin created a privileged elite, a class of citizens that endured throughout the history of the Soviet Union. People with special talents or abilities were given special treatment, such as better living quarters, travel privileges, and access to scarce luxury foods and clothing. The privileged class included not only high Party officials and skilled managers, but also musicians, writers, and athletes, whose talents would be exploited cynically for propaganda purposes.

The visibility of the highly successful elite and the NEP retreat from socialism allayed the concerns of the democratic countries of Europe over their giant neighbor's political aims. Stalin, in turn, appeared to be less fearful of violent conflict with his World War I foes. Thus while the Soviet Union recovered from that devastating conflict, there was much less talk of world revolution as Lenin, then Stalin, sought diplomatic recognition from the very countries they had once hoped would join the Russian Communists in overthrowing capitalist governments. However, Stalin continued to support the Comintern, an international organization established in 1919 to foment world revolution, until it was shut down during World War II as a concession to the Allies.

Despite the success of NEP, or perhaps because of it, by the late 1920s Stalin began to be suspicious of members of the Party who seemed insufficiently enthusiastic about his leadership and the transition from NEP to collectivization. To eliminate opposition and potential deviation from the direction he intended the country to take, Stalin embarked on the systematic removal of his political opponents, both real and imagined. Such an undertaking, defined as a purge, usually began with accusations of disloyalty to the Communist Party or other crimes, then proceeded to trial, imprisonment, and even execution.

THE PURGES

The Great Purge occurred roughly from 1934 to 1938, but Stalin conducted limited purges throughout his career. Lesser purges began in the late 1920s, about the time of Stalin's great drive to replace NEP with collectivization. Historian Nicholas Riasanovsky says of the Great Purge that it "marked Stalin's extermination of all opposition and his assumption of complete dictatorial power."[28] A number of officials, including Stalin's one-time rival Bukharin, were accused of counterrevolutionary activities and of being "right-wing deviationists" and expelled from office or from the Party altogether. In 1934, Sergey Kirov, a moderate Leningrad Party official, was assassinated, probably on Stalin's orders. Among those accused of plotting the murder were Zinov'ev and Kamenev, partners with Stalin in the ruling troika that had emerged during Lenin's final illness. Zinov'ev and Kamenev almost certainly had nothing to do with the assassination, but the event offered Stalin a convenient way to get rid of these former rivals, and they were sentenced to prison. Others accused in the plot were sent to prison camps in Siberia.

During the era of the purges, several high-ranking government officials were subjected to show trials. The first, in 1936, included Zinov'ev and Kamenev once again. Predictably, the former troika members, along with fourteen other Party officials, were convicted and executed. Two additional show trials were held in 1937 and 1938, this time claiming thirty-seven victims, including Nikolay Bukharin.

The show trials relied on elaborate "confessions" by the accused, thus eliminating the need for prosecutors to produce or fabricate physical evidence against them. The defendants, who confessed under torture, usually named additional "traitors," who were then rounded up, becoming victims of the purges as well.

The purges just prior to World War II had a devastating effect on the Soviet ability to defend the country. About half of the Soviet military officer population had been executed, jailed, or sent to labor camps in Siberia. By the time the purges wound down, millions of Soviet citizens, many of them government or Party officials, former allies or aides to Stalin himself, had been killed or jailed. The reasons

Russian workers approve the outcome of a trial—one of many that gave Stalin a way of eliminating formal rivals.

PURGED

"The main aim was to make a prisoner sign his interrogation record. Most of these people were illiterate. And so they stamped the prisoner's finger on each sheet. Those who refused had their fingers squeezed between the door and the wall until their fingers were broken.

What were the specific crimes they were accused of? In Kolpashevo [a town on the Ob River in central Siberia, site of one of the massacres of the Great Purge], for example, a plan to blow up a bridge over the Ob River. But at the time this bridge did not exist! In Tomsk, they would charge people with planning the explosion of a bridge over the Tom River, which also did not exist.

The Purge did not have to do, after all, with punishing people for actual crimes. To the extent that it had a conscious purpose, it was to inspire terror and obedience. The very impossibility of the crimes must have added a spooky dimension to that terror. To be charged with plotting to blow up a bridge that did not exist must have made people feel at the mercy not only of a cruel and powerful state, but of a frightening, incomprehensible new system of logic, against which there could be no appeal, no argument, no demonstrating that the crime you were accused of was impossible."

for the purges are still unclear. Some historians believe Stalin was mentally ill. Roy Medvedev concurs in this view:

> It is not difficult to detect pathological elements in his behavior. Morbid suspiciousness, noticeable throughout his life and especially intense in his last years, intolerance of criticism, grudge-bearing, an overestimation of himself bordering on megalomania, cruelty approaching sadism—all these traits, it would seem, demonstrate that Stalin was a typical paranoiac.[29]

Others surmise that for Stalin, the purges were the ultimate deterrent, a tactic for commanding blind, unquestioning obedience to his policies. This theory is supported by a great irony of the period. In 1936 Stalin issued a constitution that promised free elections, universal suffrage, and basic civil and economic rights for all Soviet citizens. These announced privileges were rendered worthless, however, by the stipulation that all political power was to be held by the Communist Party.

Stalin's lip service to greater freedom was a ruse to draw attention away from the actual results of his dictatorship: millions of deaths of Soviet citizens due to famine or purges, and lives of scarcity and terror for the vast majority of survivors. Stalin used a similar deception on the eve of World War II, attempting to divert German interest from the Soviet wealth in land and minerals by entering into a friendship pact with German dictator Adolf Hitler.

THE NONAGGRESSION PACT

In the late 1930s Germany began moving against its neighbors, annexing weaker countries such as Czechoslovakia and Austria. In addition, according to historian Nicholas Riasanovsky, "Germany and Japan concluded the so-called Anti-Comintern Pact [in 1936] aimed specifically against the U.S.S.R."[30] The pact called for opposition to international communism.

Stalin's response to these aggressive moves was to negotiate a secret nonaggression pact with Germany by which he hoped to head off future invasion by Germany. Under the agreement, the USSR would gain control of part of Poland after Hitler's September 1939 invasion of that country, sparking World War II. Shortly thereafter, the Soviet Union invaded Latvia, Lithuania, and Estonia, incorporating the Baltic countries, against their will, into the Soviet Union.

Stalin's pact with Hitler collapsed on June 22, 1941, when Hitler declared war on the Soviet Union as German troops were crossing the Soviet border. Stalin's purge of the officer ranks had rendered his forces woefully unready, and the Germans seized equipment, territory, and troops in the early days of the invasion. By November Hitler's army had pushed through Ukraine and begun its siege of Leningrad.

WORLD WAR II BEGINS

Stalin's efforts to build up his industrial base paid off in World War II, which the Soviets called the Great Patriotic War. Indeed, as Germans invaded the western Soviet Union, the Soviets were able to dismantle entire factories in that region and move them to safety in the north of the country. By 1943 the tide of the war turned in the Allies' favor. By the end of 1944, the Soviets had recaptured Leningrad, were able to push into Eastern Europe, and at war's end in April 1945 captured the German capital, Berlin. The Soviets joined American, British, and French forces in partitioning the defeated Germany into two spheres of influence, East (administered by the USSR) and West (jointly occupied by the United States, Great Britain, and France).

The United States wanted to restore war-torn Europe's largely destroyed industrial base as quickly as possible, and so provided massive monetary and technical aid in a recovery program known as the Marshall Plan. Although the Soviet Union

The arrival of the Russian Red Army in Berlin.

was a U.S. ally during World War II and suffered extremely heavy damage and an estimated 20 million casualties, it received no aid under the Marshall Plan. Ian Grey writes that "it may be doubted whether the U.S. Congress would have sanctioned the extension of [Marshall Plan aid] to Soviet Russia, except on terms completely unacceptable to Moscow."[31] At any rate, the Soviet Union declined to apply for Marshall Plan aid and discouraged its Eastern European allies from participating.

Stalin, contrary to the spirit of the Marshall Plan, wanted to extract as much from the defeated Germans as possible for reparations. To do so he moved entire factories from his section of Germany to the Soviet Union. These differing approaches to peace, Stalin's determination to retain control of East Germany and to "influence" (i.e., control) Eastern Europe, and the fundamental ideological conflict between communism and capitalism led to a period of Soviet-Western conflict and

world tension known as the cold war, which lasted until the collapse of the Soviet Union.

THE COLD WAR BEGINS

The cold war actually began before the end of World War II. Tensions were already building in February 1945 when Stalin met with Allied leaders Franklin Roosevelt of the United States and Winston Churchill of Great Britain. The conference, which took place on Stalin's home turf, Yalta, in the Crimea, was held to draw up plans for a peace agreement with the defeated Axis powers.

Two provisions of the agreement reached at Yalta stand out as issues aggravating the cold war: Stalin's insistence on controlling Poland's government after the war, and his undertaking to enter the war in Asia. In exchange for promised help in the Pacific theater, the Soviet Union was given control of several Japanese islands. Had Soviet plans for invading Japan not been cut short by the Japanese surrender in August 1945, the Soviets would have gained a territorial foothold in Japan. Nevertheless, Stalin wanted a role in administering postwar Japan, but this demand was refused by Harry Truman, who became president on the death of Franklin Roosevelt two months after Yalta.

Stalin's foreign policy after the war, and consequently his cold war posture, was influenced by his long-held determination to create a buffer zone between the Soviet Union and the non-Communist world. This buffer-zone view is confirmed by historian Alexander Werth, who points out that "throughout their history the open expanses of European Russia had been tempting to all kinds of invaders. . . . Almost invariably these foreign invaders came from the West—mostly through Poland; in 1941 they came simultaneously from several countries of Eastern Europe, all the way from Rumania to Finland."[32]

Control of Eastern Europe would eliminate much of this invasion threat, and thus Stalin moved to ensure domination of the East European countries along the western border of the Soviet Union.

His postwar domestic policy had two major components: to repair the destruction of the Soviet industrial base and to build a strong military force. To implement these goals, the Fourth Five-Year Plan was launched in 1946. By concentrating on industrial and military development, Stalin once again neglected the needs of the state-run agricultural system, and the consumer requirements of his industrial workers. Knowledgeable American policymakers viewed Stalin's renewed

Franklin Roosevelt (center), Winston Churchill (left), and Stalin meet in Yalta to discuss plans for a peace agreement with the defeated Axis powers.

interest in resupplying his army at the expense of his people's needs as an indication of planned future aggression.

Soviet Postwar Rearmament

Stalin's military buildup alarmed an American Soviet expert, George F. Kennan, who would later become ambassador to Moscow, and he outlined his thoughts on future U.S.–Soviet relations in a long telegram to the U.S. State Department, the substance of which he repeated in a magazine article in July 1947. Believing that Soviet expansionist ambitions posed a serious threat to the United States and to the world, Kennan proposed what became known as the "containment" policy. Robert Daniels, in the following analysis, quotes extensively from Kennan's telegram:

> The problem [of containment] . . . was compounded by Marxist suspicions of capitalist intervention and old Russian fears of the outside world, a "neurotic view of world affairs" providing "justification for that increase of military and police power of Russian state, for that isolation of Russian population from outside world, and for that fluid and constant pressure to extend limits of Russian police power which are together the natural and instinctive urges of Russian rulers."[33]

Despite his hostility to the West and the large proportion of the Soviet economy dedicated to defense, consistent with his "neurotic view of world affairs," Stalin made one last attempt to improve the Soviet economy. In 1951 he launched a five-year plan scheduled to run until the end of 1955, but he would not live to see it through.

Stalin's Death

On March 1, 1953, Stalin suffered a brain hemorrhage and died. History professor Francis Randall reports that "just before his death there were suspicious arrests of doctors and others, accompanied by rumors of a new purge of much or all of the high Party leadership."[34] The doctors' arrests were deemed suspicious because they fed rumors of a plot against Stalin's life, but no such conspiracy was ever confirmed. The doctors were eventually released, saved from being purged by Stalin's own death.

Daniel Diller, in evaluating Stalin, sums up his career:

> Stalin was an organizer, a man of action rather than a theoretician. . . . At great human cost, Stalin succeeded in making the Soviet Union an industrial giant. . . . His paranoid pursuit of absolute control led him to order the arrest and execution of many of his colleagues and contributed to the creation of a repressive system.[35]

The drama of choosing Stalin's successor began immediately after his death. Despite the assurances of Stalin's lieutenants that a new type of collective leadership would rule the nation, Nikita S. Khrushchev was already plotting his rise to power.

Chapter

4 The Khrushchev Era: 1953–1964

Nikita S. Khrushchev, the son of a miner, was born in 1894 in a small village in southwestern Russia. He was educated in a village school before joining the Communist Party in 1918. He rose to become head of the Party in Ukraine in 1938. After World War II, he was put in charge of

Nikita Khrushchev was put in charge of Stalin's agricultural reform program after World War II.

Stalin's agricultural reform program. By the time of Stalin's death he was well positioned to compete for the leadership role. However, he did not immediately become supreme leader.

It first appeared after Stalin's death that a committee of top leaders would govern jointly, with Georgy Malenkov as prime minister. In 1976 historian Roy Medvedev and his brother Zhores, a scientist exiled from the USSR for his dissident views, published this explanation of Soviet collective leadership:

> Although the principle of "collective leadership" was proclaimed after Stalin's death, the age-old tradition of the Russian nation and the thirty-five-year-old tradition of the Soviet Union demanded the rise to preeminence of a single supreme leader, firmly managing the country's affairs. After the first weeks of "collective leadership," it became obvious to an astute observer that only Malenkov, [V. I.] Molotov [Stalin's vice-premier and foreign minister], or Khrushchev had all the attributes of such a leader.[36]

Early predictions by Western observers favored Malenkov as Stalin's successor and focused attention on him, accordingly. However, Lavrenty P. Beria and Khrushchev were both contenders. Beria, head of the Soviet internal security forces, was eliminated when it was learned in 1953, shortly after Stalin's death, that he had plotted a coup to seize power for himself. Other top leaders ordered Beria's arrest and execution.

Eliminating Beria allowed the Party to gain control of the secret police, then called the MGB. (The secret police had been called many names: the Cheka, or Vecheka, under Lenin; the GPU, then the OGPU, then the NKVD. In 1954 the secret police would once again be reorganized as the KGB.) Beria's execution was important because as head of a powerful and unregulated secret police agency, he would have been able to selectively manipulate the fate of individuals within the Party, including its top leaders.

With Beria gone and Molotov's influence declining, the power struggle was between Khrushchev and Malenkov, and it centered on economics. Malenkov wanted to shift state resources toward producing more consumer goods in an attempt to relieve the persistent shortages that had plagued the country since Lenin instituted Communist rule. Khrushchev, on the other hand, wanted to continue the Stalinist policy of directing most state resources to heavy industry and the military.

At first Malenkov's push for consumer goods won the greatest support of Soviet leaders, who feared that continued shortages would lead to unrest. Khrushchev managed to gain enough support within the Central Committee of the Communist Party to reverse Malenkov's policies. At the same time, the committee forced Malenkov to resign from his powerful post as chairman of the Council of Minis-

THE BERIA AFFAIR

Mark Frankland gives Khrushchev's account of the end of the Beria affair in Khrushchev.

"[Khrushchev] told a foreign politician in 1956 that a special session of the Presidium was called at which Beria was cross-examined for four hours [about his plans for a coup]. Then Beria was left alone while his colleagues discussed what to do with him. They were convinced of his guilt, Khrushchev said, although there was 'not enough juridical evidence' to prove it. But it was impossible to let him go free, and so 'we came to the unanimous decision that the only correct measure for the defence of the Revolution was to shoot him immediately. This decision was adopted by us and carried out on the spot.'"

Shepilov, Molotov, and Malenkol (left to right), of the Council of Ministers, seen together just before their fall.

ters. Malenkov was replaced by Khrushchev's ally, Nikolay Bulganin, an old Cheka hand with a flair for economic policy. This move left Khrushchev in control of the government, although he would never have the unchallenged authority Stalin enjoyed. Khrushchev also wanted to distance himself from Stalin's rule-of-terror governing style. He therefore initiated a campaign of "de-Stalinization."

DE-STALINIZATION

The Soviet people had experienced dreadful oppression under Stalin's dictatorship, and even top Party leaders, though not forced to endure material deprivation, had lived in constant fear of arrest on irrational charges, followed by torture, a show trial, and execution. After the ruthless leader's death, Khrushchev attempted to relax tensions by means of a carefully planned series of changes called de-Stalinization.

In the initial phases of de-Stalinization, citizens were granted greater freedom of movement within the country (but not out of the country). Artists and writers also enjoyed greater freedom of expression. Thousands of political prisoners were released from gulags, extremely harsh labor camps in Siberia and elsewhere. As a result of these departures from Stalinist policies, by the time Khrushchev solidified his leadership position, in 1955, de-Stalinization had yielded considerable benefits. At the same time, Robert Daniels notes, "none of Khrushchev's reforms entailed a fundamental alteration in the institutions or the powers of the Stalinist system."[37]

The next phase of de-Stalinization, however, would amaze the free world as well as the nations of the Communist bloc. In an address to the Twentieth Soviet Party Congress in February 1956, Khrushchev denounced Stalin as a "bloody tyrant." In these startling remarks, known as "the Secret Speech," Khrushchev also

De-Stalinization was not meant to promote democracy. In Mark Frankland's Khrushchev, *the premier's adviser Fedor Burlatsky explains the Soviet belief in absolute rulers.*

"Stalin had developed Lenin's idea of a guiding Communist Party into a system that justified his absolute control over all aspects of Soviet life. And Khrushchev, too, believed that the Party should have as absolute a control over Soviet life as Stalin had exercised in his own person. . . . Accordingly in the secret speech one of Khrushchev's main concerns was to see that, despite the admission of past errors, nothing should be done to damage the Party's claim to authority."

blamed Stalin for the heavy Soviet losses of World War II. He rightly pointed out that the purges resulting in the execution of thousands of military officers had played a significant role in those losses, but he neglected to cite his own participation in the purges.

Published widely outside the Soviet Union, the Secret Speech was a secret kept only from average Soviet citizens. The new era of tolerance signaled at least in theory by the speech did not extend to freedom of information. The only people inside the Soviet Union who heard the complete contents of the speech were the leaders of the Party congress at which it was delivered and members of some local soviets, where it was read aloud in closed sessions.

Khrushchev also accused Stalin of developing a "personality cult," in which Stalin himself, elevated to the status of infallible hero-king, was attended by flatterers and yes-men instead of competent policy advisers. When Stalin died, devo-

tees of the personality cult saw to it that their hero was buried in Lenin's tomb, a Soviet shrine. Khrushchev, who had been part of the group that had originally exalted Stalin, secured the support of his coleaders to have Stalin's coffin moved from its place of honor near Lenin to another spot in the Kremlin, the vast government headquarters in Moscow. This seemingly minor gesture was, in reality, a major symbolic event, signifying yet more de-Stalinization.

KHRUSHCHEV'S FOREIGN POLICY

While de-Stalinization was occurring at home, Khrushchev began exploring a move to ease tensions abroad. The cold war continued, but Khrushchev took several steps that indicated to Western countries that the Soviet leader was willing to explore the possibility of better relations with his neighbors. Khrushchev withdrew troops from Austria, stationed there since World War II, and proposed a summit with Western leaders to be held in Geneva, Switzerland, in 1955 to discuss the reunification of Germany, disarmament, and other issues of mutual concern.

At the summit U.S. president Dwight Eisenhower suggested an "open skies" agreement, in which the United States and the Soviet Union each would allow fly-overs by the other country for aerial inspection of both superpowers' military facilities. Khrushchev rejected this proposal, but he generated some goodwill four years later when he traveled to the United States, visiting a Los Angeles factory and an Iowa farm as well as the United Nations.

Also in 1955, Khrushchev formed the Warsaw Pact, in which the states of Eastern Europe committed themselves to a twenty-year term of "friendship, cooperation, and mutual assistance."[38] The Warsaw Pact was an alliance of Eastern bloc countries to counter what the Soviets perceived as the threat from the North Atlantic Treaty Organization (NATO) alliance, the postwar mutual defense pact of Western countries. Soviet dominance of the Warsaw Pact countries was part of the long-standing buffer-zone strategy. The Eastern European countries lay between the Soviet Union and its World War I opponents, and Khrushchev and his lieutenants would be sensitive to any moves

Hungarian rebels wave their flag from a captured Soviet tank in front of parliament in Budapest.

KHRUSHCHEV TAKES OFFENSE

In 1959 Khrushchev was officially invited to visit the United States. He worried that he would not be treated well because of past tensions between the United States and the Soviet Union. In Khrushchev Remembers *he recalls his anxiety.*

"When informed by our embassy in Washington that a certain number of days in our schedule had been set aside for meetings with the President at Camp David, I couldn't for the life of me find out what this Camp David was. I began to make inquiries from our ministry [of foreign affairs]. They said they didn't know what it was either. . . . One reason I was suspicious was that I remembered in the early years after the Revolution, when contacts were first being established with the bourgeois world, a Soviet delegation was invited to a meeting held someplace called the Prince's Islands. It came out in the newspapers that it was to these islands that stray dogs were sent to die. In other words, the Soviet delegation was being discriminated against by being invited there. In those days the capitalists never missed a chance to embarrass or offend the Soviet Union. I was afraid maybe this Camp David was the same sort of place, where people who were mistrusted could be kept in quarantine."

Soviet Premier Nikita Khrushchev in New York during a thirteen-day tour of the United States.

by Warsaw Pact member states toward independence from Soviet domination.

Therefore, Khrushchev was greatly alarmed when, in 1956, Poles and Hungarians interpreted the denunciations of Stalin as a signal of relaxation of Soviet dominance of their governments. Reasoning that because of de-Stalinization they should have the opportunity to voice their grievances, the Poles rioted, demanding government reform, better living and working conditions, and civil rights. Khrushchev headed a delegation to Poland to persuade the Polish people that rebellion against Moscow would be put down by means of military invasion. Order was restored and the Polish government resumed its subservience to the Soviet Union.

More serious riots also broke out in the same year in Hungary. Several days after the visit of Khrushchev's delegation to Poland, Hungarian students demonstrated in Budapest, demanding a new government. This time the Soviets sent tanks. In the ensuing uprising three thousand people were killed and another two hundred thousand fled the country; many eventually immigrated to the United States. In the wake of the Hungarian uprising, the Soviet Union increased its attention to military defense strategies and its relations with the West.

SOVIET ARMS BUILDUP

The Hungarian uprising chilled Soviet relations with its most powerful cold war adversary, the United States. Adding to tensions in August 1957, the Soviet Union tested an intercontinental ballistic missile (ICBM) and on October 4 launched *Sputnik*, the world's first man-made satellite, into orbit. The *Sputnik* launching was an important milestone, but the Soviet government's heavy investments in atomic energy, rockets, missiles, and space travel were in stark contrast to the poor standard of living of the people. Acute housing shortages still existed in the cities, and consumers in state stores often found shelves nearly empty.

Tensions flared further when the Soviets shot down a U.S. spy plane flying over Russian territory, and a summit planned for Paris in 1960 was canceled.

After his election as president in 1960, John Kennedy met with Khrushchev in Vienna in June 1961 to discuss the future of the divided country of Germany, administered by the Allies in accordance with the terms of the German surrender at the end of World War II in 1945. Khrushchev, wanting to force the Western powers out, threatened to sign a treaty with East Germany that would make future German reunification more difficult. As Ian Grey makes clear, though, Khrushchev "misjudged the determination of Kennedy and the support he had in the West in resisting such threats."[39] The Western powers responded with a military buildup of NATO forces. The Soviets countered by building a wall separating East and West Berlin, which prevented many would-be refugees from leaving the eastern sector. Another, more serious, confrontation between the Soviet Union and the United States would occur the following year in Cuba.

THE CUBAN MISSILE CRISIS

Encouraged by Fidel Castro's successful establishment of a Communist government in Cuba in 1959, Khrushchev had hoped to use Soviet aid and influence on the Caribbean island to foment revolutionary Communist movements throughout Latin America. To that end, the Soviets began to build bases in Cuba capable of launching missiles that could strike many U.S. cities.

When this threat to American security was discovered in October 1962, President Kennedy announced a blockade of all cargo ships bound for Cuba that might contain military equipment. Word of the blockade caused several ships from Soviet-bloc nations to turn around in mid-ocean and head back to port rather than face a challenge from the U.S. military. President Kennedy also declared that any attack launched by Cuba on any nation in the Western Hemisphere would be regarded as an attack on the United States by the Soviet Union.

Khrushchev then wrote to President Kennedy, proposing a compromise: The United States would withdraw from Turkey missiles the Soviets viewed as threatening, and the Soviet Union would withdraw its weapons from Cuba. Even though the missiles in Turkey were obsolete and already scheduled for removal, President Kennedy refused to make their removal a part of the deal. Nevertheless, Khrushchev conceded and ordered the Cuban missile bases quickly dismantled. This action was regarded by other Communist leaders as a betrayal of socialism. The Chinese government criticized the move, as did Khrushchev's own Party officials. Sino-Soviet relations had seen ups and downs since the takeover of mainland China by Communists in 1949, and Khrushchev's perceived humbling in Cuba served to accelerate another downward spiral.

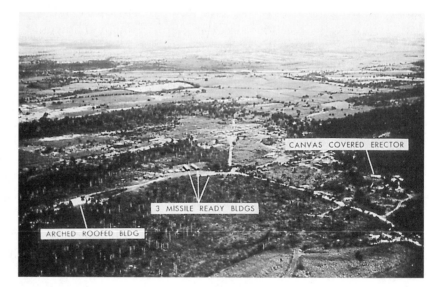

Medium-range ballistic missile bases in Cuba.

President John F. Kennedy addresses the nation on television concerning the Cuban Missile Crisis.

SINO-SOVIET RELATIONS

Khrushchev's biggest problem in dealing with China was that the Soviet Union wanted more peaceful relations with the Western world while China, an aggressive Marxist state, wanted increased confrontation between the Communist bloc and the West. Mao Zedong, the Chinese dictator, viewed U.S. support of the island of Taiwan, called Nationalist China as the site of the Chinese government in exile during the Khrushchev era, as a provocative threat to his Communist government. He believed Khrushchev's efforts to forge friendlier relations with the United States amplified the American threat to mainland China.

Khrushchev attempted to appease China's sense of vulnerability by offering a nuclear shield to protect China in case of attack. Mao Zedong preferred to have his own defenses, however, and pressed Khrushchev for technology to produce nuclear weapons. Khrushchev at first secretly agreed, but fearing that a Chinese-U.S. confrontation would involve the Soviet Union, he repudiated the agreement in 1959. In his memoirs Khrushchev describes the Soviets' generous treatment of China: "Before the rupture in our relations, we'd given the Chinese almost everything they asked for. We kept no secrets from them. Our nuclear experts cooperated with their engineers and designers who were busy building an atomic bomb. We trained their scientists in our own laboratories."[40]

Despite the Soviet-Chinese split, Khrushchev wanted to influence the emerging nations in Asia and Africa by providing technical aid along with propaganda designed to promote communism in those countries.

SOVIET AID TO AFRICA AND INDIA

The period between Stalin's death in 1953 and Khrushchev's forced retirement in 1964 was a time of anticolonial and independence movements throughout the Third World. Nationalist sentiment grew in Europe's former colonies in Africa, Asia, and Indonesia. Khrushchev regarded these emerging nations, newcomers to international politics, as ideal prospects for establishing Communist societies.

For example, India had gained independence from Britain in 1947 but in the mid-1950s was struggling to gain political and economic stability. Khrushchev visited India in 1955 and promised substantial economic aid, which by 1960 amounted to more than had been given China. The Soviet Union also agreed to produce its MiG-21 jet fighter in India, an apparent show of favoritism that further exacerbated tensions between China and the Soviet Union.

In Africa, Khrushchev developed several show projects in newly independent countries, former colonies, the Congo, Guinea, and Kenya, in hopes of promoting Communist takeovers of those countries. These demonstration projects failed, however. Soviet planners had neglected to consider the technological backwardness of the client states, and they had not committed sufficient military forces to shore up their client governments against rival groups hoping to achieve power.

Because of his misadventures in Africa, the failure to maintain an armed presence in Cuba, and the growing distance from China, and despite some generally positive initiatives to promote coexistence with the United States, Khrushchev's colleagues in the Soviet leadership regarded his foreign policy as a failure. His agricultural initiatives fared little better.

ATTEMPTS TO REFORM: THE VIRGIN LANDS PROGRAM

In 1954 Khrushchev sent his protégé Leonid Brezhnev to Siberia and central Asia. Brezhnev, a tough technocrat who was also a veteran of the campaign to eliminate the kulaks, was not being exiled. Instead, he was charged with implementing a program Khrushchev had

WHY DID VIRGIN LANDS FAIL?

Khrushchev's Virgin Lands project to cultivate millions of acres of Siberian land to alleviate chronic food shortages was considered a failure. Khrushchev's own insightful words, from Khrushchev Remembers: The Last Testament, *provide some explanation.*

"The problem of transportation took time to solve. For a long time the harvested grain was simply piled up in the fields. We didn't even have enough sacks to carry the wheat, and our trucks were inadequate, too. The roads were so bumpy that much of the crop was strewn along the side and lost. . . . Among the problems that came up, certain regions which had been designated for cultivation turned out to be barren. But often such setbacks could be rectified. There was enough land in Kazakhstan so that when one stretch proved infertile, we would simply mark it off and look for a new stretch."

developed to solve the Soviet Union's chronic agriculture shortages.

This ambitious project, called the Virgin Lands Program, succeeded in planting grain on more than 100 million acres of previously uncultivated land. But although the program relieved temporary grain shortages between 1954 and 1960, harvests were generally poor and the Soviet Union ultimately resumed importing large amounts of grain from Canada, Australia, and the United States. There were several reasons for the failure of the Virgin Lands project: It was difficult to recruit workers to move to uninhabited areas; transportation facilities for moving the harvest were inadequate; and unanticipated bad weather frequently led to crop losses.

Another of Khrushchev's reform plans was to decentralize industry and establish regional authorities away from Moscow. However, the government bureaucracies, those most vulnerable to the proposed reforms, were able to block these plans, and instead supported a plan to overthrow him.

KHRUSHCHEV SURVIVES OUSTER PLOT

Khrushchev's efforts at decentralization of economic planning and his demotion of several powerful government ministers, including Georgy Malenkov and even Nikolai Bulganin, Khrushchev's hand-picked premier, inspired opponents to attempt to overthrow him in June 1957. The conspirators, who became known as the anti-Party group, wanted to force Khrushchev's resignation and be able to advise the Central Committee, which was domi-

nated by Khrushchev supporters, that their leader had stepped down. Khrushchev refused to resign and demanded a vote by the committee, which he won. One of Khrushchev's advisers, Fedor Burlatsky, describes the accumulating anti-Khrushchev feeling:

> The events in Hungary triggered an explosion of feelings that had been building up within the Soviet leadership. [A faction of longtime Party members who remained loyal to Stalin's memory] had compiled a long list of grievances over Khrushchev's innovations in domestic and foreign policy, decided to move into the attack and remove him as party leader in one fell swoop.[41]

The attempt failed, however, for the plotters had not reckoned on Khrushchev's considerable support in the Central Committee and in the army. Khrushchev then forced the active conspirators from their Presidium (formerly called the Politburo) and Central Committee seats. At the same time, he promoted his supporters to fill the posts of ousted members. Khrushchev then had a freer hand to pursue his policies unimpeded. Many bureaucrats and political leaders threatened by these policies drew support until they were sufficiently strong to successfully challenge Khrushchev's authority.

KHRUSHCHEV'S FALL

Unlike Lenin and Stalin, Khrushchev never wielded absolute power. Nor did he report to the Soviet people, who in any event had no say in selecting their leaders. Khrushchev remained as supreme leader of the Soviet Union only as long as his allies in the Presidium and the Central Committee outnumbered his enemies. However, the days when political opponents could be arrested and exiled or even executed had ended with the death of Stalin. Khrushchev's opponents, and those he demoted or fired, had remained unexecuted and unexiled, and some maintained influence within the Party.

By 1964 Khrushchev's mistakes and failures had reached a critical mass. His foreign policy blunders and domestic failures could no longer be excused on grounds of blind loyalty. Perhaps the most serious domestic failure was his ef-

By 1964, Khrushchev's failures could no longer be excused and he was forced to resign.

fort to reorganize the highly centralized economic control system into two subsystems. Daniel Diller describes this reform as a

> split of most of the lower party and governmental organs into two independent structures. One was industrial (or urban), the other agricultural (or rural). The industrial regional party committees and soviets . . . supervised nearly all the population in the cities. . . . The agricultural counterpart supervised rural citizenry and institutions. . . . This bifurcation [two-way split] failed largely because it created needless confusion and threatened or diminished the jobs of many powerful bureaucrats and administrators.[42]

Furthermore, as Diller concludes, "Khrushchev's attempt to reorganize the party and government in 1962 was probably the domestic initiative that most damaged his standing."[43]

On October 15, 1964, the Central Committee announced that, because of advanced age and failing health, Khrushchev had requested to be relieved of his duties. This was a lie. The Presidium of the Central Committee had requested his resignation. It was a humiliating dismissal, but Khrushchev could take comfort in knowing that in an earlier age he would have been taken out and shot.

Leonid Brezhnev, who had been in charge of the disastrous Virgin Lands initiative, was named first secretary of the Communist Party, and Aleksey Kosygin was named premier.

5 The Brezhnev Era: 1964–1982

Leonid Brezhnev was born in 1906 in Ukraine. Trained as an engineer, he joined the Communist Party in 1931. He served in the military in World War II, and afterward held several important Party posts before being elected to the Central Committee in 1957. He was one of Khrushchev's fa-

Leonid Brezhnev became first secretary after Khrushchev resigned.

vorites, and he was elected chairman of the Presidium of the Supreme Soviet in 1960. Brezhnev became first secretary, or general secretary, after Khrushchev's ouster in 1964.

SCRAMBLE FOR LEADERSHIP

Just as the Stalin and Khrushchev eras began with governing committees in power instead of clear individual successors, the Brezhnev era began with tentative roles for several leaders. Aleksey Kosygin was named premier, or head of state, and Brezhnev was named general secretary of the Communist Party. Because the Communist Party controlled the state, however, Party chief Brezhnev was able to wield more power than Premier Kosygin.

Other members of the Party leadership limited Brezhnev's power, and he never managed to dominate government policy. He ruled as a member of an oligarchy, meaning he shared power with several others, including Mikhail Suslov and Nikolay Podgorny, members of the Politburo with wide influence, and Premier Kosygin. Brezhnev was, however, the member of the oligarchy most visible to

BREZHNEV OFFENDS THE ARMY

Zhores Medvedev, in his biography Andropov, *said he believed that the army was disillusioned with Brezhnev because of his exaggerated claims of heroism during World War II, which he bolstered by awarding himself medals.*

"The top military commanders were certainly irritated by the exaggeration of Brezhnev's wartime role. They knew what was usually required for the award of these decorations, and were deeply offended when Brezhnev awarded himself the Order of Victory. . . . It was intended only for field commanders of whole fronts or groups of fronts who had successfully planned and executed large-scale battles. . . . By presenting it to himself he devalued military decorations in general."

the outside world because, as general secretary, he was regarded as first among equals.

Like Khrushchev and Stalin before him, Brezhnev secured his power base, placing trusted associates in positions of influence and power throughout the government. He also maintained a leadership style quite different from that of his predecessors, described by Khrushchev adviser Fedor Burlatsky:

Brezhnev's main trait as political leader was revealed in the first months of his rule. An extremely cautious man, who had not taken a single rash step in his rise to power, Brezhnev adopted a centrist position from the very start. . . . In effect, he followed a tradition that had taken effect after Lenin's death. Not everyone is aware that Stalin also came to power as a centrist.[44]

BREZHNEV LEADERSHIP EMERGES

As general secretary, Brezhnev was responsible for relations with other Communist governments, while Kosygin was responsible for relations with non-Communist governments. Kosygin was also responsible for economic planning, and he revised and scaled back to more realistic goals a seven-year plan Khrushchev had initiated in 1959. These new goals included shifts toward defense buildup and heavy industry.

De-Stalinization was slowed and partially reversed when positive references to Stalin began to appear in speeches and the government-controlled media. Khrushchev's more permissive attitude toward artists and writers was reversed and all writers, artists, and performers were expected to adhere to official artistic guidelines drawn up by Party officials.

The more far-reaching of policy reversals was the abandonment of Party reforms reflecting Khrushchev's ineffective attempts to separate planning functions into separate agriculture and industry sectors and to begin decentralizing the bureaucracy. Brezhnev's economic policies would favor military over domestic needs. However, Zhores Medvedev points out that the desired military buildup of the 1970s and early 1980s failed to materialize: "By 1979, however, the army had become very critical of Brezhnev's leadership. A strong army cannot coexist with a weak economy and poor agriculture performance."[45] To fulfill the needs of the military, Brezhnev turned his attention to the economy.

Aleksei Kosygin's goals included a defense buildup and expansion of heavy industry.

ECONOMIC POLICY

Never a particularly creative leader, Brezhnev tackled economic policy by launching yet another five-year plan (1966–1970). Good weather helped spur economic growth in the agricultural sector in the late 1960s, which in turn boosted other areas of the economy, including industry. As a result, the standard of living began to rise, but the good times did not last long. Burlatsky explains the economic stagnation during Brezhnev's military buildup:

> During [the Brezhnev era] Japan became the second industrial power in the world, South Korea followed on the heels of Japan, and Brazil became one of the new centres of industrial power. True, we [the USSR] gained military parity with the most advanced industrial power in the modern world. But at what a price! The price was increasing technological backwardness in all other areas of the economy, and the further destruction of agriculture.[46]

In the 1970s, bad weather, always a specter in Russia's harsh climate, returned to plague agriculture, creating food shortages. At the same time, popular dissatisfaction with the harshness of Soviet life, lack of opportunity, and the failure of central planning began to show itself in such social problems as widespread alcoholism.

In the 1970s the problems due to food shortages were exacerbated by the poor planning that characterized Soviet history. Hunger and resentment of perceived injustices contributed to a decline in individual well-being during the Brezhnev era. As a result of the downward spiral of living standards, which fifty years after the revolution had not attained Western standards, economic growth slowed throughout the 1970s. The declining economy would make Brezhnev's foreign policy ambitions more difficult.

BREZHNEV'S FOREIGN POLICY

Though Brezhnev and other Soviet leaders endorsed Khrushchev's policy of peaceful coexistence, relations between the United States and the Soviet Union began to decline after 1965, largely due to tensions over the Vietnam War.

North Vietnam's rocket units were responsible for bringing down many U.S. planes.

The Vietnam War posed a dilemma for the Soviet Union. North Vietnam, an ally of the Soviet Union and China, was at war with South Vietnam, which was heavily supported, financially and militarily, by the United States. Brezhnev and Kosygin wanted to send military aid and supplies to North Vietnam, but were reluctant to further antagonize the United States. On the other hand, withholding aid would offend the Chinese, who felt that the Soviet Union, as the largest of the socialist economies, should take the lead in supporting North Vietnam.

At the same time, the Chinese refused permission for Soviet aircraft to use Chinese bases to transfer supplies to North Vietnam. Daniel Diller quotes a Chinese newspaper story explaining that "If we were to take united action [i.e., help the Soviets help the North Vietnamese] on the question of Vietnam . . . wouldn't we be helping them [Brezhnev and Kosygin] to bring the question of Vietnam within the orbit of Soviet-U.S. collaboration."[47] In other words, the Chinese worried that the Soviets would not take a sufficiently hard line against the United States in the conflict, perhaps even electing to side with the United States against China.

The Chinese were also concerned that helping the Soviets help North Vietnam would enhance the Soviet image in the eyes of Third World countries, where the Soviet Union and China vied for dominant influence. The tensions between the Soviet Union and China would continue until the U.S. withdrawal from Vietnam in the mid-1970s; however, Vietnam was not the only contentious issue between the two countries.

Middle East Policy and the "Spirit of Glassboro"

Soviet influence in the Middle East was at first shattered in 1967 after the Six-Day War between Israel and hostile neighboring Arab states. The stunning Israeli victory demonstrated, among other things, the inferiority of the military equipment the Soviets had supplied to their Arab clients. Several Arab states, including Egypt, broke off diplomatic relations with the United States in retaliation for U.S. support of Israel, however, and the Soviet Union stepped back into the picture, helping to resupply the armies of Egypt, Syria, and Jordan.

Shortly after the Six-Day War, Premier Kosygin met with President Lyndon B. Johnson in Glassboro, New Jersey, to discuss tensions in the Middle East and the problems of nuclear arms proliferation. The "Spirit of Glassboro" that developed between the two leaders resulted in the drafting of a nonproliferation treaty. Johnson and Kosygin signed the treaty in 1968, but no other nuclear power followed suit. Moreover, while the Senate was considering ratification, the Soviet Union invaded Czechoslovakia and support for the treaty dwindled.

The Soviets Invade Czechoslovakia

The Soviet invasion of Czechoslovakia in August 1968 was in response to a liberalization movement in the Czech government expanding freedoms of speech, assembly, and religion and granting greater tolerance of opposing political parties. These reforms threatened Socialist rule. The Soviets justified the action by alleging that the Czech government had asked for aid to put down an uprising. Both Czech government and Communist Party leaders, however, protested Soviet presence on Czech soil and denied having requested the troops.

To create an appearance of mutual consultation, Moscow then invited Czech leaders to a conference in Moscow to discuss the contradiction of Soviet philosophy represented by Czechoslovakia's emerging ideas of "social democracy," with multiple parties competing for power. Brezhnev, Kosygin, and other Soviet representatives traveled to the Czech border town of Cierna. Czechoslovakia was represented by First Secretary Aleksandr Dubcek and other members of his government. After the meeting the Soviets appeared to be satisfied with Czech leadership and agreed to withdraw their troops; however, in late August 1968, the Soviets sent four hundred thousand troops into Czechoslovakia to put down what the Soviets described as a counter-revolution. Nicholas Riasanovsky believes the Soviets were motivated to invade "by fear for the Warsaw Pact which the Czechs wanted to modify although not abandon . . . [and] by the concern lest liberalism at home [Soviet Union] be too much encouraged."[48]

Dubcek was arrested and persuaded to end the Czech liberalization movement. The following year he was replaced with a pro-Soviet hardliner who crushed all remnants of the liberalization movement.

Czech leaders, such as Aleksandr Dubcek (third from left) at a conference in Moscow to discuss the contradictions of Soviet philosophy.

The Czech encounter resulted in the Brezhnev doctrine, established to prevent similar independence movements.

THE BREZHNEV DOCTRINE

The Brezhnev doctrine was announced in 1968 to justify far-reaching Soviet intrusion into the internal affairs of other Socialist states, especially in Eastern European states that shared a border with the Soviet Union. The purpose of such Soviet interference was to prevent modification of the Marxist-Leninist form of government so firmly advocated by the USSR. The doctrine was rationalized in terms of the long-standing buffer-zone strategy to slow invasion from the USSR's traditional European enemies.

The Brezhnev doctrine went farther than assuring a buffer zone between the USSR and potential invaders from Western Europe. It encompassed all Socialist states, and stated simply that the Soviet Union and its allies would intervene, militarily if necessary, in any conflict in a Socialist country that threatened to overthrow or even modify an existing Socialist system. The doctrine carried the strong suggestion that any change in a Socialist government that was unfriendly to Moscow, regardless of whether that nation's form of socialism was changed, would result in Soviet intervention.

The Czech invasion, along with Brezhnev's statement that the Soviet Union was prepared to prevent any state, once having chosen a Communist government, from declaring independence, set back Soviet relations with the West. During this time, Richard Nixon was campaigning for the U.S. presidency on a platform that included establishing better relations with the Communist world, the so-called policy of détente.

DÉTENTE

Nixon's idea of détente simply meant the relaxation of tensions between nations, very much like Khrushchev's idea of "peaceful coexistence," and his détente efforts produced an arms limitation agreement with the Soviets. Détente was pursued by Presidents Gerald Ford and Jimmy Carter.

Trade relations improved between the two superpowers with increased Soviet purchases of U.S. grain, but soured when U.S. policymakers, including members of Congress, objected to Soviet treatment of dissidents. Nevertheless, Carter and Brezhnev signed the second Strategic Arms Limitation Treaty (SALT) in 1979. The Soviet invasion of Afghanistan a week later ended U.S. support for détente, however. The Soviets invaded because they hoped to take advantage of an Afghani political upset to install a puppet leader loyal to Moscow. Thus despite

U.S. president Jimmy Carter and Soviet president Leonid Brezhnev sign the second Strategic Arms Limitation Treaty.

evidence to the contrary, the invasion was "hailed by the Soviets as a true popular democratic revolution."[49] The United States responded by instituting trade sanctions against the Soviet Union and also withdrawing from the Summer Olympics scheduled for Moscow in 1980.

The election in 1980 of conservative Republican Ronald Reagan as president of the United States dashed hopes for resumption of détente in the near future. But as the hard-line anti-communist took

Lech Walesa led a strike against the increase in meat prices.

office, a crisis was building in Poland that would test Soviet resolve in imposing the Brezhnev doctrine.

LECH WALESA AND POLISH SOLIDARITY

In August 1980 a strike at Lenin Shipyard in Gdansk, Poland, erupted over hikes in the price of meat. Lech Walesa, a shipyard worker, led the strikers—who named their union Solidarity—in their demand for recognition of independent labor unions and the right to strike. First Secretary Edward Gierek, leader of the Polish Communist Party, not only granted these demands but promised strikers increased wages and better medical services and food in exchange for returning to work.

Although Gierek was shortly afterward ousted for giving in to strikers' demands, his replacement promised to honor the agreement with the strikers. He also pledged to maintain close ties with the Soviet Union, leading to fears of Soviet intervention. Then in September the government repudiated the month-old strike settlement, and the strike resumed and simmered until December 1981, when martial law was declared and the leaders of Solidarity, including Walesa, were arrested and briefly imprisoned.

Brezhnev, citing the Brezhnev doctrine, persuaded the Polish government to violate the new pact with Solidarity by enacting a law banning strikes. To emphasize his concern, Brezhnev sent troops to hold maneuvers near the Soviet-Polish border, seeming to ignore warnings against direct intervention by outgoing U.S. president Carter.

Robert Daniels calls the U.S. reaction to the Afghan and Polish crises the New Cold War, in which a "resurgent conservatism led Americans to perceive the Soviet Union as a revolutionary and expansive evil, with which there could be no trusting coexistence or lasting accommodation."[50] Indeed, Ronald Reagan called the Soviet Union the "evil empire."[51]

President Reagan imposed trade sanctions on both the Soviet Union and Poland, which had cooperated with the Soviets by breaking the strikes, but he placed most of the blame for the crisis on the Soviet Union. The sanctions stopped the export of food to Poland and oil and gas equipment to the Soviet Union, while restricting air service and port privileges to both countries. During this period Brezhnev, in deteriorating health, was becoming increasingly inattentive to the affairs of the country. His inattention, along with economic stagnation, fed an alarming growth in corruption and black market activities, both of which had long been problems in the Soviet Union.

Russian citizens experienced glaring discrepancies in living standards. Only the elite could afford goods such as television or have access to choice living quarters.

Soviet Corruption Is Widespread

The sluggishness of the Soviet system fed a general economic vulnerability to corruption. Because economic planning for every aspect of Soviet life originated in Moscow, and because goods and services were allocated by government bureaucrats rather than through market mechanisms, the cumbersome economic system provided abundant opportunities for bribery. Indeed, the inefficiencies built into the centralized system encouraged this corrupt practice. All over the USSR, bureaucrats diverted the choicest goods and services, both for personal gain and to use as bargaining chips to trade for favors. By the Brezhnev era, corruption was so widespread that many of its manifestations were accepted as routine. Shop managers and bureaucrats, for example, were particularly likely to divert merchandise away from state stores to sell on the black market. They did not always carry out thefts personally, but they brokered or permitted them, and they took their cuts.

Brezhnev was acquainted firsthand with the workings of the black market: "You don't know what life is like," he chided a speechwriter after he became general secretary. "Nobody lives on their wages. I remember in my youth when I was studying at the technical college we earned extra money by unloading freight trains. How did we manage? Three bags of a container would go to [whoever had paid for the merchandise] and one to us. That's how everyone lives in this country." According to Burlatsky, Brezhnev also regarded the black market as normal, "as well as thieving in the service sector and bribes to bureaucrats."[52]

Members of the elite were able to shop in special stores that provided goods not available to ordinary citizens. In Moscow, where frequently two or more families shared an apartment because of a chronic housing shortage, officials with influence could obtain choice living quarters. Government expense accounts allowed these fortunate civil servants to build vacation homes.

In a country that officially advocated equal treatment of all citizens, glaring discrepancies between the living standards of government and Party officials and ordinary people had a corrosive effect on morale at all levels of society. Thus the government made a show of concern about such criminal activity. Indeed, some

charges of theft and fraud against the state carried the death penalty. Even so, examples of corruption became increasingly outrageous.

CORRUPTION AND THE BLACK MARKET: TWO CASES

A deputy in the Ministry of Fisheries was sentenced to death for his part in a scam in which the managers of a fish cannery disguised cans of expensive caviar with labels for cheap herring in order to divert the caviar into the black market. Zhores A. Medvedev, in *Andropov,* a biography of Brezhnev's successor, explains how this fraud worked: "These tins of herring were distributed to specially selected restaurants in Sochi [an exclusive Black Sea resort town] and other places, and shipped abroad where they were repacked in small caviar tins and sold as caviar through accomplices in the Soviet foreign trade network. In the restaurants the tins were recorded as herring, but they were sold as caviar and the extra cash was not registered."[53] The cannery managers split the illicit proceeds of this fraud with the restaurant managers.

Hedrick Smith, *New York Times* bureau chief in Moscow in the 1970s, devotes an entire chapter in his book *The Russians* to corruption and the black market. He reports dozens of anecdotes he labels as typical and routine examples of corruption in every aspect of Soviet life. For example, Smith once gave a pair of nearly impossible-to-get world hockey championship tickets to a Soviet friend, thinking

FALSE IMPRESSIONS OF DEMOCRACY

The role of the Communist Party in the governance of the Soviet Union was deliberately obscured. The Soviet propaganda machine, in the form of radio and television newscasts, helped perpetuate the myth that the government was independent of the Party. In an essay, "Radio Moscow's North American Service," taken from Ladislav Bittman's The New Image-Makers, *Igor Lukes explains how Radio Moscow tried to create the false impression that the Soviet Union's government resembled Western democracy.*

"Virtually all news segments on Radio Moscow's North American Service begin with a reference to the Soviet government. . . . One can hear news about '1,500 delegates to the legislature of the USSR.'. . . The government will sometimes allude to the existence of a serious 'debate' that allegedly preceded the conclusion of the Soviet legislature's business.

This observation may seem trivial, but one must consider that all decision-making power in the Soviet Union is vested in the hands of various organs of the Central Committee of the Soviet Communist Party. The primary mission of governmental institutions, such as the Supreme Soviet and the USSR Council of Ministers, is merely to supervise the implementation of party instructions. The secondary purpose of the Soviet government is to project to the outside world the illusion that the Soviet Union is a country more or less similar to Western democratic countries."

---

the recipient of the gift would enjoy the event. Instead, the friend gave the tickets to the woman who managed a large Moscow food store, explaining to Smith that much as he would have enjoyed the game, it was critical to his family that the executive be periodically rewarded, lest she cut off his access to the hard-to-get goods: "She sells us our best food." This manager of a government-owned shop removed the best goods from the shelves to sell privately, leaving customers unwilling or unable to pay black market prices

to pick over the sparse, inferior leftovers. "She is terribly rich," Smith's friend continued, "because people pay her extra money for such things."[54]

Corruption was rampant long before the Brezhnev era, but it seemed to flourish more openly, and it grew to epidemic proportions, during Brezhnev's leadership. Brezhnev largely ignored corruption; reform-minded Russians looked to his successor, Yuri Andropov, for solutions. Brezhnev's death would present an opportunity for reform.

THE DEATH OF BREZHNEV

Leonid Brezhnev died of a heart attack in November 1982 at the age of seventy-five. He had been the top Soviet leader for eighteen years, a term exceeded only by Stalin's twenty-nine years. Daniel Diller sums up Brezhnev's era of corruption, noting his penchant for self-promotion: "His writings were widely published . . . his picture appeared on billboards and at official events . . . and his military service during World War II was glorified."[55]

Another elderly Politburo member, Yuri Andropov, replaced Brezhnev as first secretary. Zhores Medvedev sets the scene for the surprise selection of the former KGB head:

> Andropov's selection was a surprise: If the news of Brezhnev's death was received without emotion by the Soviet public, Andropov's election met with no enthusiasm. The first gloomy anecdote to circulate was probably an accurate reflection of the general feeling: Andropov explains to a foreign journalist that he is sure the people will follow him. "And those who don't follow me will follow Brezhnev."[56]

AND THE DEATH OF ANDROPOV

Andropov died in January 1984, fifteen months after taking office. During his short tenure, he began to address the charges of corruption that were so prominent during the Brezhnev era. He also proposed a series of economic reforms such as decentralizing the economic planning system and giving more responsibility to regional bureaucrats, all ideas reminiscent of Khrushchev's reform efforts.

Medvedev emphasizes the difficulty of implementing reforms in his 1983 book describing the succession from Brezhnev to Andropov:

> But the replacement of the top ruling group cannot take place very quickly in the Soviet Union, for the system works on the basis of general consensus among the leading members of the Central Committee and the government, not through free elections at regular intervals which can change the composition of the party in power or replace it altogether.[57]

Nevertheless, Andropov's program was implemented to a limited degree and was considered a success.

AFTER ANDROPOV

Andropov was succeeded by another former secret police official, Konstantin Chernenko, who died in March 1985 without making any major changes in initiatives begun by Andropov. The death of three elderly leaders, part of a Politburo sometimes called the "gerontocracy," or "rule by old men," increased calls for new blood in the Kremlin. Convinced that it was time to find a younger leader, the day after Chernenko's death the Party bosses turned to fifty-four-year-old Mikhail Gorbachev, the youngest member of the Politburo, to become the new general secretary.

The older generation of Soviet leaders, the heirs of the Bolsheviks of 1917, had produced a government that was dysfunctional in many respects. To have any hope of continuing in modern times, the system required far-reaching reform. Burlatsky identifies some of the problems:

> The main lesson to be learned from the Brezhnev era was the failure of the command-administrative system which had taken shape under Stalin. Not only did the state not promote progress; rather, it increasingly hampered the economic, cultural and moral development of society. . . . Structural reforms and *perestroika* [restructuring] were indisputably the logical way out of stagnation.[58]

The new leader, Mikhail Gorbachev, would try to implement these reforms.

Chapter

6 The Gorbachev Era: 1985–1991

Mikhail Gorbachev, proclaimed first secretary of the Communist Party so soon after Konstantin Chernenko's death, was born March 2, 1931, in the Stavropol region in southwestern Russia. The son of peasants, he began moving toward a career in the Communist Party as a young man, dri-

Mikhail Gorbachev appointed young, reform-minded people to positions of power.

ving a combine harvester on a state farm while participating in Komsomol (the Young Communist League). Gorbachev received a law degree in 1955 and rose through Party ranks to hold several important regional posts, became a member of the Central Committee in 1971, then a member of the most important governing organ in the Soviet Union, the Politburo, in 1979. As the youngest member of the Politburo at a time when the country needed to replace the gerontocracy with younger blood, Gorbachev was in an ideal position to be chosen as supreme leader.

Zhores Medvedev provides historical context for the opening days of the Gorbachev era:

> In Stalin's time change was closely associated with methods of coercion and terror. The enormous machine of repression became the most important instrument of the personal power of the General Secretary. Khrushchev, on the other hand, ruled primarily through the Party apparatus. . . . A new, inflexible, tenured Party and government elite began to take shape and form a privileged ruling class. . . . [This class] inhibited social, economic

Gorbachev and President Ronald Reagan discuss limits on weapons inventories.

and cultural renewal and it [in the later Brezhnev years] finally degenerated into a gerontocracy.[59]

Thus one of Gorbachev's first moves was to appoint younger, reform-minded people to the Politburo and to government ministries, and to begin to refocus on the reform movement begun by Chernenko's predecessor, Yuri Andropov. The KGB leader who was briefly head of state had helped Gorbachev in his rise to the Politburo, and now the younger man would attempt to carry out his mentor's vision.

THE BROADCAST ERA PENETRATES SOVIET SECRECY

The necessity for reform was at least partly the result of greater public aware-ness of the corrupt behavior of leaders and bureaucrats. This was made possible by the improvement in communications technology. Before the advent of mass media of radio and television, which, like other technological advances came late to the Soviet Union, the government was able to effectively control the dissemination of information to the country and thus was able to shape perceptions of life both in and out of the Soviet Union.

Radio and television changed all that. Despite the best efforts of the government to jam radio and TV broadcasts, a picture of life outside the Soviet Union got through to the Soviet people. Besides, people could look around them and see for themselves the results of increasing corruption. Corruption created differences in the living standards of the government and Party elite from those of ordinary people. The necessity for ordinary citizens to participate in the black market to obtain essential goods and the widespread knowledge of these inequities, made possible by better mass media technology, could no longer be ignored. Reform would be the new leader's first priority.

Another early priority for Gorbachev was to repair strained relations with the United States to slow the arms race. Soviet determination to maintain weapon equity with the much richer United States had long been a financial drain on Soviet resources. Gorbachev wanted to reduce his country's need for expensive weapons, as well as the maintenance of a highly trained military force able to use them. To this end, he met with U.S. president Ronald Reagan at a summit in Iceland in October 1986. Some progress was made at this meeting for limiting weapon inventories, but the talks broke down over the issue of weapons testing. Nevertheless, a path to better relations was established and Gorbachev turned to other pressing matters:

economic stagnation and increasing public agitation for greater freedom. Soon two words began appearing regularly around the world in press accounts of Gorbachev's reform plans: "perestroika," meaning restructuring, and "glasnost," meaning openness.

PERESTROIKA

Gorbachev, the father of perestroika, is frequently portrayed as the architect of the breakup of the Soviet Union and the collapse of communism in Eastern Europe, but that was never his intent. Nevertheless, the reforms he advocated set in motion a series of events that led inevitably to that outcome. Daniel Diller places perestroika in perspective: "The perestroika debate challenged other central tenets of socialism, such as bans on private property and income equality. . . . [Gorbachev's] reforms fell far short of the

The needs of ordinary citizens sparked the growth of industry such as this auto works factory in Moscow.

economic overhaul that most Western observers believed was necessary to turn around the Soviet economy."[60]

Until the beginning of perestroika in the mid-1980s, efforts to improve Soviet life through increasing industrial and agricultural production had only addressed superficial flaws in the centralized planning system necessitated by a Socialist economy. No one questioned the basic premise of central planning, but earlier reforms were only Band-Aids; they ignored the root causes of socialist economic failure, such as the cumbersome planning and bureaucratic controls that prevented efficient operation of any enterprise. To demonstrate how the Soviet economy was supposed to work—and how it failed—the editors of *Soviet Union: A Country Study* describe the functioning of a typical Soviet industry:

> Planners [of the construction of an electric power plant] relied on timely delivery of turbines from a machine plant, whose planners in turn relied on timely delivery of semifinished rolled and shaped metal pieces from a metallurgical combine [a specialty shop]. Any change in specifications or quantities required approval by all the ministries and intermediate planning bodies in the power, machine, and metallurgical industries—a formidable task under the best of circumstances.[61]

From this description it is easy to see how one small failure or delay anywhere in a major industrial process could short-circuit the whole. In a free-enterprise economy, breakdowns in a complex system are quickly remedied—perhaps a missing item is acquired from one of many competing vendors. Not so in a centrally planned system, where competition by multiple suppliers is ruled out of the production process by definition.

The shortcomings of the Soviet central planning system were evident as early as the Lenin era: The New Economic Policy had reintroduced a limited level of free enterprise among the lower economic strata. NEP was considered a great success, but because it violated Marxist ideology, it was dropped after the late 1920s. Every Soviet leader, from Lenin to Brezhnev, insisted loudly that he was dedicated to eradicating all vestiges of private enterprise in favor of centralized economic planning and state ownership of all means of economic production. Despite the success of free-market capitalism, showcased worldwide in nations as diverse as the United States and the tiny Caribbean island nation of Grenada, the Soviets stuck to the notion that free markets spelled disaster. Zhores Medvedev offers one version of this unusual viewpoint:

> While the "planners" are in favor of better organization and more power for administrators, the "social economists" advocate some liberalization and the legalization of freelance activity in some sectors. They understand that competition and the market can provide a stimulus. The "planners," on the other hand, believe that modern computer technology can take millions of variables into account and

Since the Soviet Union has imported grain throughout most of its history, efforts to improve agricultural production were an attempt to meet everyday consumer needs.

perfect the economic plans. Free competition and market-oriented production will, they think, create waste and redundancy.[62]

The Marxist belief that free-market competition creates waste and redundancy was at the heart of shortages throughout the history of the Soviet Union. Medvedev's "planners" consistently failed to produce sufficient goods—or even basic necessities—for the Soviet people. All the five-year plans and all the forced collectivization throughout the Stalin, Khrushchev, and Brezhnev eras were not able to feed the Soviet population, let alone satisfy consumer needs of housing and everyday consumer goods. The Soviet Union, with a large portion of the earth's fertile agriculture land, imported grain almost throughout its history. By the time Gorbachev was named general secretary, ordinary Soviet citizens were beginning to privately question the Soviet system. Government officials who harbored doubts refrained from voicing them.

During Andropov's brief tenure, people had begun to quietly talk about the need for radical reforms to raise the country out of its malaise of corruption and economic decline. Gorbachev, as Andropov's protégée, was determined to put the ideas about reform into practice through perestroika. To gain public support for such radical departure from Marxism-Leninism, Gorbachev chose to implement a policy of greater openness, or glasnost.

GLASNOST

Glasnost, the policy that permitted open discussion of—and criticism of—government policy opened the gates to an unstoppable flood of criticism and discussion of the state, the Communist Party, and the country's leaders. As Raymond Zickel recalls in *Soviet Union*, "Editors, journalists, and other writers transformed newspapers, journals and television broadcasts into media for investigative reports and lively discussions of a wide variety of subjects that had been heavily censored before 'glasnost.'"[63]

Runaway glasnost was not what Gorbachev had in mind, and the government tried to backpedal by restricting criticism through censorship, but it was too late. Daniel Diller writes:

Gorbachev introduced this concept into the political discourse in early 1985. He maintained that glasnost was inextricably linked with perestroika because economic reforms would not work unless they were supported by broad public participation and enthusiasm. . . . [In addition] the power of the corrupt and intransigent bureaucracy to block or stall significant changes would have to be broken.[64]

The argument for free-market economics was more than just an ideological debate about the direction of economic policy. It was also a struggle for control of the nation's considerable wealth, which included immense stretches of farmland, oil and coal reserves, and even valuable urban infrastructure. Journalists Dusko Doder and Louise Branson explain that

the hard-line party bureaucrats who practically "owned" the state-run economy had no intentions of surrendering without a fight. For a regional party boss, district party secretary, or city party chief, glasnost was one thing, wealth another. They had become used to controlling this wealth, the output of mines, factories, and forest lands, and they were deeply dug in, more deeply than Gorbachev had expected them to be.[65]

Nevertheless, glasnost and perestroika created an optimistic atmosphere, and people began to imagine a free society. Once everyone began talking freely it became impossible to control the free flow of information. Previously, only a few dissidents had dared speak, and it was relatively easy to hunt such dissidents down and arrest or intimidate them. But now, with everyone speaking freely, and the whole world watching, terror tactics on a large scale were no longer possible.

While this new freedom was breaking out in Moscow, people in some of the republics were becoming restless and began to talk about independence. This general desire for independence took on practical urgency in May 1986 when the news got out that a serious nuclear power plant accident had occurred the month before in the Ukrainian city of Chernobyl, releasing harmful radiation into the atmosphere and forcing the evacuation of thousands of inhabitants.

The government's delay in admitting the accident seemed to validate the growing criticism of the central government and to justify talk of independence. Daniel Diller believes that "the Chernobyl nuclear disaster in April 1986 marked a turning point in the glasnost campaign because it illustrated to the Soviet leadership why freer information was important."[66] The head-in-the-sand avoidance of responsibility for the defects that caused the accident also put both workers at the

The government's delay in admitting to the nuclear disaster at Chernobyl sparked much criticism.

plant and nearby residents at unnecessary risk.

Election Reform

To ease the growing dissatisfaction with and criticism of the central government, in 1988 Gorbachev proposed to cut back the power of the Communist Party by limiting terms of office for Party and government officials. The same proposal called for the election of legislators by se-

cret ballot. However, these elections were not to be like those in a Western-style democracy. As Gail Sheehy demonstrates, not every victor in the May 1989 election to the Congress of People's Deputies owed his or her seat to direct popular election, as this term is understood in the West:

> In truth, those spring elections were far from the Western principle of "one man, one vote"; Gorbachev's variation was to give ordinary people one vote, while the Party elite had two or three. A full third of the "People's Deputies" seated at the 2,250-member congress were not elected by the people at all, but nominated instead by trustworthy "public" organizations mostly controlled by the Party.[67]

Many people, especially in the West, thought Gorbachev's reforms were a back-door method for ending communism in the Soviet Union, but Gorbachev has always denied this. Indeed, as Daniel Diller observes: "[Gorbachev] had staunchly upheld the validity of Marxist ideology and the necessity of Communist Party control of society."[68] However, limited free-market characteristics were introduced into the economy and controls on information were loosened. Though Gorbachev consistently reaffirmed his allegiance to the Soviet Union's Communist system, his reforms would ultimately be its undoing.

Gorbachev eventually achieved passage of most of his perestroika proposals, creating a national elected legislature, the Congress of People's Deputies, and persuading this body to approve a Western-style presidency and cabinet form of government for the Soviet Union. He then persuaded them to elect him as the first president, an office with powers far broader than those of the old ceremonial presidency, a post most recently held between 1985 and 1988 by Andrey Gromyko, a survivor of the Stalin era. Yet the Soviet economy was still performing poorly, and the more liberalized political atmosphere emboldened miners in Siberia to strike, demanding more money and more political autonomy.

INDEPENDENCE MOVEMENTS

With unrest in Russia and the other republics spiraling out of control, the Eastern European states Moscow had dominated since World War II began to behave more independently. This trend was inaugurated in September 1988 when thousands of East Germans began fleeing the country, and in 1989 with elections in Hungary and Poland. Bernard Gwertzman summarizes the unraveling of the Soviet empire:

> By the end of the year, all the former members of the Soviet bloc had in one way or other done away with the ruling Communist Party and their close links to Moscow. Rumania, which was independent of Moscow, also came apart. Gorbachev's response was almost nonchalant.[69]

By 1990 the independence movement among the non-Russian republics of the Soviet Union was well under way. In March, Lithuania formally withdrew from the Soviet Union and installed a

Miners strike in Mezhdure-chensk. Unrest in Russia initiated independence movements in other countries.

Lithuanians volunteer to defend their newly independent republic.

non-Communist government. Only a few years earlier Soviet troops would have been dispatched to the rebellious republic, but Gorbachev responded by applying a boycott against Lithuania, cutting off goods and supplies.

The boycott was ineffective, and, although there was scattered military action throughout the rest of 1990, the failure of Moscow to immediately quell the independence movement by means of armed force encouraged others to demand an end to the monopoly of power held by the Communist Party. In early 1991, too late to be effective, Soviet troops invaded Lithuania. The delay, in part a result of the diversion of leadership's attention to the growing reform crisis, emboldened the Lithuanians. Despite the presence of Red Army troops, Lithuanians voted overwhelmingly for independence. Meanwhile, trouble was brewing in the Russian Republic.

THE BREAKUP BEGINS

On May 30, 1990, Boris Yeltsin was elected president of Russia. Less than two weeks later, the parliament of the Russian Republic proclaimed that Russian law took precedence over Soviet law, a complete reversal of seventy-two years of Soviet dominance over the constituent republics within the Union of Soviet Socialist Republics.

By July 1991, Gorbachev, in an effort to prevent the breakup of the Soviet Union, unveiled a plan to share power with the republics. This plan proposed expansion of market economies, religious freedom allowing the formation of new religious groups, and most important, an end to Communist Party monopoly of power. The proposal drew wide support except for Communist bureaucrats, whose positions were threatened. Army officials were also opposed to power sharing: David Pryce-

Jones says that "Devolution of power from the centre to the republics threatened the very existence of the Red Army."[70] Further complicating matters, the newly almost-independent republics were beginning to form military units of their own. Thus many young men avoided being drafted into the Red Army but readily enlisted in the military services of their national republics.

On July 31, a few days after the plan was approved, Gorbachev met in Moscow with U.S. president George Bush, to sign a nuclear arsenals pact designed to achieve a reduction in the strategic nuclear forces of both countries. This was the Strategic Arms Reduction Treaty (START), which mandated reduction in the strategic arms stockpile of both the United States and the Soviet Union. After the Bush meeting, Gorbachev left for a fateful vacation in the Crimea. While he was on vacation, Communist opponents of his program would attempt to take over the government.

THE COUP D'ETAT

On August 18, 1991, while at his vacation house in the Crimea, Mikhail Gorbachev was visited by a delegation of Party leaders who demanded that he leave office. They placed him under house arrest, cut off from all outside contact, then broadcast an announcement to the country that Gorbachev was ill and unavailable for comment. Francis X. Clines, in a *New York Times* article, describes the next ominous step: "Vice President Gennadi I. Yanayev was assuming presidential powers under a new entity called a State Committee for the State of Emergency. Its members include Vladimir A. Kryuchkov, chief of the KGB. and Dmitri T. Yazov, the defense minister."[71] The coup occurred a few days

Russian president Boris Yeltsin rallies demonstrators protesting the attempted overthrow of Gorbachev.

before Gorbachev was to have signed an agreement allowing the nation's republics greater autonomy. The pending agreement raised the stakes for those who feared Gorbachev was destroying the Soviet Union as well as for those in the republics looking for greater autonomy. The agreement would have given the republics greater say in administering their own affairs.

This agreement was of special interest to Boris Yeltsin, the former Moscow mayor who was elected president of the Russian Republic in 1990. Yeltsin had been seeking greater autonomy from the Soviet Union, and the autonomy agreement would legitimize his efforts. Yeltsin

was determined that the coup should not succeed because, if the antireformers seized power, the autonomy agreement would be rescinded. He issued an order putting Soviet government agencies under Russian control.

Over the next several days, uncertainty and chaos gripped Moscow. Although initially military leaders were divided, slowly high-ranking officers and troops in the streets turned against the coup, and after four days it fizzled. Instrumental in defeating the coup was Boris Yeltsin, whose heroic public defiance rallied crowds in the streets and finally convinced the plotters that they could not win. Gorbachev was restored to office.

Gorbachev and President George Bush sign a pact designed to reduce the supply of nuclear weapons in both countries.

A MOST DRAMATIC EVENT

Some observers regard the breakup of the Soviet Union as the most dramatic event of the twentieth century. In an op-ed piece in the Boston Globe *on December 27, 1991, staff writer H. D. S. Greenway expresses that opinion.*

"It is a story of such magnitude that few have been able to capture its essence. . . .

The collapse is more than the break up of the 74-year-old Soviet Union, or even the 19th century empire of the Czars. It is more than the end of the Russia that Peter the Great consolidated in the 18th century.

It is as Mikhail Gorbachev said: a thousand years of history that was discarded this week. Few will miss the Soviet Union of the last 74 years, least of all those who lived under its monstrous tyranny. The experiment in social engineering that Vladimir Illych Lenin unleashed upon the world in November of 1917—especially when you add in the excesses of his disciples, Stalin, Mao and Pol Pot—caused more misery and murder than any other political movement in this century. . . .

The aspirations of Mikhail Gorbachev, who wanted to reform his country but keep it intact, have gone for naught. Will he be remembered as a transitional figure who was, ultimately, unable to either comprehend or control the forces that had been loosened—alongside Alexander Kerensky who took over from the Czar only to lose to the Bolsheviks? It may seem so to him now. A sense of failure and regret came through his Christmas Day abdication speech—especially in his sorrow over his people 'ceasing to be citizens of a great power.' Certainly, if man in the street interviews can be believed, the former Soviet peoples consider him a failure."

The coup attempt by Communist Party leaders convinced Gorbachev that the Party could no longer be trusted, and on August 24, just six days after the coup attempt, he resigned as Party leader. He was, of course, still head of state as the Soviet president—a post he did not resign—and he made one more attempt to patch up the crumbling union. The attempt would fail: One by one, the Soviet republics declared their independence, and by December 21, 1991, all the republics except Georgia had issued a proclamation stating that the Soviet Union no longer existed.

After the Fall

The breakup of the Soviet Union was amazingly swift. When Gorbachev resigned the presidency on December 25, 1991, the Soviet Union was no more. Casual observers in the West often assume that Boris Yeltsin was Gorbachev's successor, but that is technically not so, since Yeltsin was never president of the Soviet Union. For all practical purposes, however, the Russian Republic, which Yeltsin has headed since 1991, is the successor to the defunct Soviet state. Thus many of the popular assumptions about the role of Yeltsin in the post-Soviet era have some merit.

THE RUSSIAN REPUBLIC TAKES OVER SOVIET ASSETS

The new non-Soviet Russian state inherited the Red Army and most stockpiles of Soviet weapons. Russia inherited the Soviet foreign policy establishment with its outstanding treaties and its foreign embassies throughout the world. For the most part, foreign states' ambassadors to the Soviet Union became ambassadors to Russia. After all, the foreign embassies were all in Moscow, the Russian as well as Soviet capital.

By far the largest of the fifteen republics in the union, with more than half the population, and with by far the greatest landmass, Russia was always the engine driving the government. It contained the capital, with its vast state bureaucracy and military command. It housed the lion's share of Soviet academic and scientific resources, which maintained the country's aerospace program and vast nuclear arsenal. Nevertheless, Russia contains dozens of non-Russian ethnic groups speaking non-Russian languages, maintaining non-Russian cultures with non-Russian histories: About 50 percent of the Soviet Union's 285.7 million inhabitants are non-Russian. As Bohdan Nahaylo and Victor Swoboda point out, "[A]part from the 15 nationalities in the Soviet Union which have their own fully fledged republics, there are dozens of other ethnic groups, both large and small. The languages, customs and histories of these peoples vary immensely."[72]

Many of the other republics have large populations of ethnic Russians, most of whom do not speak the local languages and did not need to when Russian was the dominant language of the entire union. These ethnic Russians were frequently resented during Soviet rule because they tended as a class to snub the local population. Now that ethnic Russians form minorities in most of the republics, many may be expected to immigrate to Russia, even if they have never been there.

REPUBLICS WITHIN THE RUSSIAN REPUBLIC

The new Russian constitution recognizes the reality of ethnic diversity by granting some measure of autonomy to twenty-one internally independent ethnic republics and other autonomous regions, districts, and cities located in the Russian Federation. Some regions, such as Chechnya, have made attempts to break away from Russia, but their efforts were at first brutally put down. Russian troops entered Chechnya in December 1994 and, after more than two months of bloody fighting, captured and destroyed the capital, Grozny. A counteroffensive by the Chechnyans in August 1996 resulted in expulsion of the Russian invaders. Chrystia Freeland, a Western journalist, describes these Red Army troops as "Moscow's drunken, unfed and ill-disciplined youths." She continues: "Chechnya's separatist fighters did more than win their own sovereignty. They proved to Russia and to the world that the Kremlin no longer had the strength to

Chechen fighters ride a captured Russian tank through the ruins of Grozny.

hang on even to its peripheral possessions."[73]

The other fourteen republics of the former Soviet Union share many of the problems faced by the Russian Republic. Russia, Ukraine, Kazakhstan, and Belarus all inherited nuclear armaments. Except for Russia, the republics lack the technology to maintain or launch the weapons. The missiles and warheads pose dangers as they are subject to theft by criminal elements and sale to rogue nations, or perhaps terrorist groups.

THE NEW NON-SOCIALIST ECONOMY

Other problems associated with the breakup include disentangling the system of central economic planning that had been run from Moscow. Some republics with factories within their borders may be cut off from materials and supplies that come from other republics. Some agricultural regions that practiced one-crop farming may find themselves with an oversupply of that crop—cotton, for example—and no grain or consumer goods.

A whole new trading system must be developed and implemented, and each new republic must create its own monetary system. Many bureaucrats in the old Soviet Union survived the breakup to secure positions of importance within their newly independent republics. Many of these former Communists have been hostile to democracy, perhaps an indication that they have not abandoned their Communist ideology. According to history professor Stephen Batalden, "In much of Central Asia and Transcaucasia, as well as in other European republics, the continuity in political leadership has been accompanied by a retreat from democratization."[74] New rulers have used the apparatus of the security police they inherited from the Soviet Union to enforce repressive measures.

For example, Soviet gold reserves were looted by officials and bureaucrats entrusted with their care in the aftermath of the breakup. David Pryce-Jones reports that KGB chairman Kryuchkov had advised the Soviet Congress in 1990 that 12 billion rubles had been smuggled out of the country. "That was an understatement," comments Pryce-Jones. "In April and May 1991 shipments of Soviet gold variously reported at between 1000 and 2000 tons reached the West. . . . Investigators had traced Soviet flight capital to accounts in almost eighty banks worldwide, with investments in hotels and property and businesses."[75]

The looting did not end in 1991. Arnaud de Borchgrave, an editor-at-large for the *Washington Times*, wrote in 1997 that

> In March, Mr. Yeltsin launched his sixth campaign in as many years against organized crime and its high-ranking protectors. He ordered all his ministers and senior officials to submit a list of all their personal assets. Country dachas and modest local bank accounts were harmless enough to disclose, but foreign bank accounts invariably were concealed. Russia's Central Bank recently authorized the transfer abroad of $800 million to pay

the country's most pressing bills. Within two weeks, Swiss banks alone had received $8.5 billion from Russia, according to the head of a large Swiss financial institution. An estimated $150 billion has left the country since 1992. . . . Benjamin A. Gilman, New York Republican, the chairman of the House International Relations Committee, calls Russia "virtually a full-fledged kleptocracy [government by thieves]."[76]

In addition to stanching the outward flow of capital, the new republics had to

The Russian vice squad undergoes training for responding to all kinds of crime and emergencies.

undertake the difficult task of privatizing industry and property once owned by the state. One of the major problems of privatization of state-owned enterprises has been that profitable or efficient enterprises that might have benefited the state were easier to privatize and were disposed of quickly. The unprofitable enterprises, such as equipment manufacturing that, because of inferior technology, cannot find an export market and are a drain on the treasury, still have not been sold. The Russian government continues to subsidize them for fear that the unemployment resulting from shutdowns would make a bad situation worse.

And indeed, factory workers are not the only ones in danger of losing their jobs. According to Chrystia Freeland, "The Russian government plans to dismiss more than 200,000 state employees. . . . [T]he drastic job cuts—including 68,000 teachers and 22,000 medical staff—were part of a sweeping plan to fire 10–15 percent of the federal government's employees."[77] The prospect of such mass firings promotes fear and uncertainty in the general population, and this atmosphere, in turn, is a breeding ground for further corruption.

A NEW CRIMINAL CLASS: THE RUSSIAN MAFIA

Much former state property has found its way into the hands of former Soviet Communist officials. A new name began to be heard throughout the former Soviet Union, especially in the industrialized sector, mafia, named for its resemblance to crime organizations in the United States and Europe. Many in the West assumed that organized crime was a new phenomenon, but "mafia" is just a new name for an old practice. Soviet corruption had already turned many officials, factory managers, and even small shopkeepers and taxi drivers into petty criminals. When the Soviet Union disintegrated they simply continued their activities, albeit with greater freedom and frequently on a larger scale.

With many repressive aspects of the Soviet system gone, self-interest became a prominent guiding principle. The Soviet Union lacked the mediating institutions that created a respect for the rule of law and moderated antisocial behavior: Labor unions, family businesses, civic associations, charities, religious institutions, and independent news media were weak or altogether absent. Notions of private property and providing for one's family

through inheritance, which would have been helpful in establishing conventions of good citizenship, had been out of favor in the Soviet Union since 1917. The situation was not much better in Eastern Europe.

DEMOCRACY IN EASTERN EUROPE

While the former Soviet republics were struggling with their new identities and new problems, the countries of Eastern Europe that had been under the control of the Soviet Union also struggled with newfound freedoms. The Berlin Wall came down in November 1989, and East and West Germany were formally reunited in October 1991. Former Soviet satellites such as Hungary, Bulgaria, and Czechoslovakia threw out their Communist governments and established democracies. Romania not only threw out its Communist dictator, Nicolay Ceausescu, but tried

Unprofitable enterprises that could not be privatized have not been shut down because of fears of unemployment.

PREDICTING THE FALL

Although the breakup of the Soviet Union surprised even well-informed people in the West, including the U.S. Central Intelligence Agency, it was not without its prophets. As quoted in *The Strange Death of the Soviet Empire*, Vladimir Bukovsky, a dissident living in London, told David Pryce-Jones in the 1980s that as more and more people challenged the system, "by 1990 at the latest the whole repressive mechanism would have ceased to function and a democracy would take its place."

him and his wife and executed them in front of television cameras.

Debate about why the Soviet Union collapsed will continue for many years to come. Essayist John P. Maynard argues that socialism destroyed itself:

> Over the years, the USSR government, which produced nothing, grew and grew and grew, while the residual productive forces steadily deteriorated. This is another of the principal reasons behind the collapse: the deterioration to the point of near total destruction of the ability to produce. What happened is most aptly described in the old Soviet joke, "They pretend to pay us and we pretend to work." The Soviet Union failed because in the end there were no producers left.[78]

Others believe Gorbachev himself, through his policy of glasnost, hastened the collapse. Essayist Michael Mandelbaum, reflecting on the consequences of educating the populace, writes that "the people of the Soviet Union were able for the first time to speak the truth about their history and their lives. . . . It began to undo the enduring effects of the terror that the Communist Party had routinely practiced during its first three decades in power."[79] The continuing drama of Soviet collapse will continue to play out for many years. Few are making predictions about the eventual outcome, but the Russian people and the people of the newly independent republics are trying to fashion Western-style democracies with free markets and the rule of law. The world waits and watches.

Notes

Introduction: On the Eve of the Revolution

1. John Bergamini, *The Tragic Dynasty: A History of the Romanovs.* New York: G. P. Putnam's Sons, 1969, p. 336.

2. Joel Carmichael, *A Cultural History of Russia.* New York: Weybright and Talley, 1968, p. 204.

3. Daniel Diller, *Russia and the Independent States.* Washington, DC: Congressional Quarterly, 1993, p. 28.

Chapter 1: The Revolution of 1917

4. Jonathan Sanders, *Russia 1917: The Unpublished Revolution.* New York: Abbeville Press, 1989, p. 29.

5. William Henry Chamberlin, *The Russian Revolution: 1917-1918: From the Overthrow of the Czar to the Assumption of Power by the Bolsheviks.* New York: Grosset & Dunlap, 1967, p. 76.

6. Richard Pipes, *The Russian Revolution.* New York: Knopf, 1990, p. 313.

7. Pipes, *The Russian Revolution,* p. 302.

8. Pipes, *The Russian Revolution,* pp. 385–86.

9. Robert V. Daniels, *Russia: The Roots of Confrontation.* Cambridge, MA: Harvard University Press, 1985, p. 129.

Chapter 2: The Lenin Era: 1917–1924

10. Ian Grey, *The First Fifty Years: Soviet Russia 1917–67.* New York: Coward-McCann, 1967, p. 117.

11. Daniels, *Russia,* p. 113.

12. Diller, *Russia and the Independent States,* p. 36.

13. Pipes, *The Russian Revolution,* p. 609.

14. Diller, *Russia and the Independent States,* p. 36.

15. Quoted in Pipes, *The Russian Revolution,* p. 791.

16. Pipes, *The Russian Revolution,* p. 796.

17. Daniels, *Russia,* p. 114.

18. Pipes, *The Russian Revolution,* p. 674.

19. Robert Payne, *The Life and Death of Lenin.* New York: Simon & Schuster, 1964, p. 536.

20. Payne, *The Life and Death of Lenin,* p. 538.

21. Diller, *Russia and the Independent States,* p. 41.

22. Roy A. Medvedev, *Let History Judge: The Origins and Consequences of Stalinism.* New York: Knopf, 1972, p. 22.

23. Louis Aragon, *A History of the USSR: From Lenin to Khrushchev,* trans. Patrick O'Brian. New York: David McKay, 1962, pp. 220–23.

Chapter 3: The Stalin Era: 1924–1953

24. Medvedev, *Let History Judge,* p. 140.

25. Raymond E. Zickel, ed., *Soviet Union: A Country Study.* Washington, DC: Library of Congress, 1991, p. 67.

26. Quoted in Adam Ulam, *Stalin: The Man and His Era.* New York: Viking, 1973, p. 291.

27. Grey, *The First Fifty Years,* p. 237.

28. Nicholas V. Riasanovsky, *A History of Russia,* 2nd ed. New York: Oxford University Press, 1969, p. 557.

29. Medvedev, *Let History Judge,* p. 306.

30. Riasanovsky, *A History of Russia,* p. 570.

31. Grey, *The First Fifty Years,* p. 417.

32. Alexander Werth, *Russia: The Post-War Years.* New York: Taplinger, 1971, pp. 61–62.

33. Quoted in Daniels, *Russia,* p. 224.

34. Francis B. Randall, *Stalin's Russia: An*

Historical Reconsideration. New York: Free Press, 1965, p. 291.

35. Diller, *Russia and the Independent States*, p. 304.

Chapter 4: The Khrushchev Era: 1953–1964

36. Roy A. Medvedev and Zhores A. Medvedev, *Khrushchev: The Years in Power.* New York: Columbia University Press, 1976, p. 6.

37. Robert. V. Daniels, *Russia: The Roots of Confrontation.* Cambridge, MA: Harvard University Press, 1985.

38. Quoted in Paul Dukes, *A History of Russia: Medieval, Modern, and Contemporary.* New York: McGraw-Hill, 1974, p. 293.

39. Grey, *The First Fifty Years*, p. 462.

40. Nikita Khrushchev, *Khrushchev Remembers: The Last Testament,* trans. Strobe Talbot. Boston: Little, Brown, 1974, p. 268.

41. Fedor Burlatsky, *Khrushchev and the First Russian Spring.* New York: Charles Scribner's Sons, 1988, p. 93.

42. Diller, *Russia and the Independent States*, p. 78.

43. Diller, *Russia and the Independent States*, p. 78.

Chapter 5: The Brezhnev Era: 1964–1982

44. Burlatsky, *Khrushchev and the First Russian Spring*, p. 215.

45. Zhores A. Medvedev, *Andropov.* New York: W. W. Norton, 1983, p. 104.

46. Burlatsky, *Khrushchev and the First Russian Spring*, p. 224.

47. Quoted in Diller, *Russia and the Independent States*, p. 85.

48. Riasanovsky, *A History of Russia*, p. 619.

49. Daniels, *Russia*, p. 350.

50. Daniels, *Russia*, p. 327.

51. Quoted in Zickel, *Soviet Union*, p. 418.

52. Quoted in Burlatsky, *Khrushchev and the First Russian Spring*, p. 223.

53. Medvedev, *Andropov*, p. 140.

54. Quoted in Hedrick Smith, *The Russians.* New York: Quadrangle, 1976, p. 84.

55. Diller, *Russia and the Independent States*, p. 97.

56. Medvedev, *Andropov*, p. 111.

57. Medvedev, *Andropov*, p. 115.

58. Burlatsky, *Khrushchev and the First Russian Spring*, p. 225.

Chapter 6: The Gorbachev Era: 1985–1991

59. Zhores A. Medvedev, *Gorbachev.* New York: Norton, 1986, p. viii.

60. Diller, *Russia and the Independent States*, p. 110.

61. Zickel, *Soviet Union*, p. 492.

62. Medvedev, *Gorbachev*, pp. 190–91.

63. Zickel, *Soviet Union*, p. xxii.

64. Diller, *Russia and the Independent States*, p. 110.

65. Dusko Doder and Louise Branson, *Gorbachev: Heretic in the Kremlin.* New York: Viking, 1990, p. 244.

66. Diller, *Russia and the Independent States*, p. 110.

67. Gail Sheehy, *The Man Who Changed the World: The Lives of Mikhail S. Gorbachev.* New York, HarperCollins, 1990, p. 275.

68. Diller, *Russia and the Independent States*, p. 108.

69. Bernard Gwertzman and Michael T. Kaufman, eds., *The Decline and Fall of the Soviet Empire.* New York: Times Books, 1991, pp. xvii–xviii.

70. David Pryce-Jones, *The Strange Death of the Soviet Empire.* New York: Henry Holt, 1995, p. 405.

71. Quoted in Gwertzman and Kaufman, *The Decline and Fall of the Soviet Empire*, p. 384.

Epilogue: After the Fall

72. Bohdan Nahaylo and Victor Swoboda, *Soviet Disunion: A History of the Nationalities Problem in the USSR*. New York: Free Press, 1989, p. xi.

73. Chrystia Freeland, "Russia: From Empire to Nation State," *Financial Times*, July 15, 1997.

74. Stephen and Sandra Batalden, *The Newly Independent States of Eurasia: Handbook of Former Soviet Republics*. Phoenix: Oryx, 1993, p. xiv.

75. Pryce-Jones, *The Strange Death of the Soviet Empire*, p. 385.

76. Arnaud de Borchgrave, "Ignoring Russia's Crisis of Crime," *Washington Times*, July 25, 1997, p. A19.

77. Chrystia Freeland, "Russia Plans to Cut 200,000 State Jobs," *Financial Times*, March 25, 1998.

78. John P. Maynard, "Soviet Communism Collapsed on Its Own," in William Barbour and Carol Wekesser, eds., *The Breakup of the Soviet Union*. San Diego: Greenhaven Press, 1994, p. 22.

79. Michael Mandelbaum, "Political Reforms Caused the Collapse of the Soviet Union," in Barbour and Wekesser, *The Breakup of the Soviet Union*, p. 46.

Glossary

Bolsheviks: A faction of the Russian Social Democratic Labor Party, later an autonomous party led by Lenin, victors in the Russian Revolution; later named the Communist Party.

Brezhnev doctrine: Soviet policy of preventing, by force if necessary, any Communist nation from replacing its government with one hostile to the Soviet Union; established after the Soviet invasion of Czechoslovakia in 1968.

capitalism: A term that has come to mean a free-enterprise economic system. Originally a Marxist term meaning an economic system in which "owners of the means of production," or capitalists, exploit the labor of workers for profit.

Cheka: The first of the Soviet secret police organizations, in operation from 1917 to 1922.

collectivization: Forcible consolidation of individual farms into state-owned cooperatives.

communism: A socialist economic system in which the means of production, e.g., all commercial enterprises, are owned in common and controlled by the state; another name for Marxism.

Cossacks: Cavalry soldiers from Ukraine and southern Russia, absorbed into the Russian army in the eighteenth century.

Duma: An advisory council to the czar and, later, a legislative body.

general secretary: Head of the Communist Party; presided over the Politburo and was usually de facto supreme leader of the Soviet Union.

glasnost: Openness; allowing public discussion of government policy; instituted by Gorbachev as part of his reforms.

Gosplan: Shortened Russian name for the State Planning Commission established in 1921, responsible for five-year plans.

intelligentsia: Intellectual class consisting of cultural, academic, and political elites.

Julian calendar: The calendar used in Russia until 1918, when the new Bolshevik government adopted the Gregorian calendar used by most of the Western world.

KGB: Committee for State Security; secret police.

kulak: A rich peasant, or any peasant farmer who used hired labor; after forced collectivization in the late 1920s, any peasant who opposed collectivization.

Marshall Plan: A U.S. aid package to the countries of Western Europe to help them recover from World War II; the Soviet Union refused to participate.

Marxism: Political ideology developed by Karl Marx (1818–1883); see **communism**.

Menshevik: A faction of the Russian Social Democratic Labor Party that believed in achieving socialism gradually; often in conflict with the Bolshevik faction.

New Economic Policy (NEP): From 1921, a partial return to a free market system for peasant farmers and other small enterprises; ended when Stalin's collectivization drive began in 1929.

Party Congress: Largely ceremonial assembly convened every five years; delegates from all the Soviet republics met to record their approval of government actions.

perestroika: Restructuring; Gorbachev's plan for reforming government and economic functions.

Politburo: Political Bureau of the Central Committee of the Communist Party; policymaking body for the Soviet Union; called Presidium during Khrushchev era.

Presidium: See **Politburo.**

purges: Period in the 1920s and 1930s in which masses of people were arrested and imprisoned or executed based on vague rumors or unsubstantiated accusations.

Red Terror: From 1918 to 1920, unrestrained police activity by the Cheka in which people were arrested and executed without justification or trials; used by Lenin to discourage opposition.

socialism: An economic and political system in which economic enterprises are either owned or controlled by the government. See also **communism.**

soviet: An advisory council; the basic government organ at all levels of the Soviet Union.

Virgin Lands: Failed agriculture program by Khrushchev in which about 70–100 million acres of uncultivated land were planted in crops.

war communism: From 1918 to 1920, Lenin's policy to quickly convert the economy to communism by ruthlessly suppressing resistance.

Whites: During the civil war, opposition to the Bolsheviks, consisting of former czarist officers and moderates opposed to Bolshevik rule.

For Further Reading

Deborah Adelman, *The "Children of Perestroika" Come of Age: Young People of Moscow Talk About Life in the New Russia.* Armonk, NY: M. E. Sharpe, 1994. Adelman interviews young Russians in their late teens about their experiences during the last decade of the Soviet Union.

Moshe Brawer, *Atlas of Russia and the Independent Republics.* New York: Modern Library, 1995. With the breakup of the Soviet Union, all maps and atlases needed to be updated. More than maps, this work describes the republics with text on demographics and geography. Charts and graphs.

Paul Dukes, *A History of Russia: Medieval, Modern, and Contemporary.* New York: McGraw-Hill, 1974. A short, complete, easy-to-read history.

Stephen Handelman, *Comrade Criminal: Russia's New Mafiya.* New Haven, CT: Yale University Press, 1995. Handelman was Moscow bureau chief for the *Toronto Star* in the early 1990s. He interviewed both criminals and ordinary noncriminal citizens.

Anatol Lieven, *The Baltic Revolution: Estonia, Latvia, Lithuania and the Path to Independence.* New Haven, CT: Yale University Press, 1994. Lieven was a journalist in the Baltics at the time of the breakup. He traces the history of the region from ancient times to the present.

Ellen Mickiewicz, *Changing Channels: Television and the Struggle for Power in Russia.* New York: Oxford University Press, 1997. The effects of television coverage of the last days of the Soviet Union. Boris Yeltsin is quoted as saying, "Television saved Russia."

R. R. Milner-Gulland et al., *Cultural Atlas of Russia and the Former Soviet Union.* New York: Checkmark Books, 1998. This atlas covers the regional cultures in maps, text, and illustrations.

Richard Pipes, *A Concise History of the Russian Revolution.* New York: Knopf, 1995. The abridged and updated version of Pipes's classic two-volume history of the revolution.

Henri Troyat, *Daily Life in Russia Under the Last Tsar.* Trans. Malcolm Barnes. Palo Alto: Stanford University Press, 1979. The author describes sights and sounds of daily life in prerevolutionary Russia, detailing the life of peasants and workers as well as the gentry and royalty.

Major Works Consulted

Louis Aragon, *A History of the USSR: From Lenin to Khrushchev*. Trans. Patrick O'Brian. New York: David McKay, 1962. A readable but unremarkable narrative of Soviet history through the early Khrushchev years.

Stephen and Sandra Batalden, *The Newly Independent States of Eurasia: Handbook of Former Soviet Republics*. Phoenix: Oryx, 1993. The Bataldens have assembled useful statistics and other demographic data on the geography, population, climate, and production of the republics of the former Soviet Union.

Fedor Burlatsky, *Khrushchev and the First Russian Spring*. New York: Charles Scribner's Sons, 1988. Burlatsky accompanied Khrushchev on many of his journeys around the world, and enjoyed his confidence.

William Henry Chamberlin, *The Russian Revolution: 1917–1918: From the Overthrow of the Czar to the Assumption of Power by the Bolsheviks*. New York: Grosset & Dunlap, 1967. First published in 1935, a comprehensive, authoritative early history of the revolution.

Daniel Diller, *Russia and the Independent States*. Washington, DC: Congressional Quarterly, 1993. An excellent short history of the Soviet Union, amazingly detailed considering its brevity.

Dusko Doder and Louise Branson, *Gorbachev: Heretic in the Kremlin*. New York: Viking, 1990. An interesting look at Gorbachev the politician.

Mark Frankland, *Khrushchev*. New York: Stein and Day, 1967. A good biography of Khrushchev, written while his fall was fresh on the minds of the observers Frankland consults.

Chrystia Freeland, "Russia: From Empire to Nation State," *Financial Times,* July 15, 1997, NewsBank NewsFile Collection. The *Financial Times* has been on the spot in the Soviet Union and its writers have astutely observed events as they happened.

Ian Grey, *The First Fifty Years: Soviet Russia 1917–67*. New York: Coward-McCann, 1967. A prominent historian, Ian Grey has produced a major work that has stood the test of time.

Bernard Gwertzman and Michael T. Kaufman, eds., *The Decline and Fall of the Soviet Empire*. New York: Times Books, 1991. A recent look at Soviet history; the authors have attempted to understand the Soviet empire's fatal flaws.

David Hoffman, "All Work, No Pay Leaves Russians Feeling Helpless," *Washington Post,* March 29, 1998. NewsBank NewsFile Collection. Hoffman was one of the many journalists on the spot as events continued to unfold after the breakup.

Nikita Khrushchev, *Khrushchev Remembers: The Last Testament.* Trans. Strobe Talbot. Boston: Little, Brown, 1974. One should always view autobiographies with caution; however, Khrushchev explains himself very well.

Roy A. Medvedev, *Let History Judge: The Origins and Consequences of Stalinism.* New York: Knopf, 1972. The Medvedev brothers have been important participants in recent Soviet history, and their perspective, though not unbiased, is valuable.

Roy Medvedev and Zhores A. Medvedev, *Khrushchev: The Years in Power.* New York: Columbia University Press, 1976. An excellent political study of the Khrushchev years.

Zhores A. Medvedev, *Andropov.* New York: W. W. Norton, 1983. A close observer, Medvedev discusses Andropov's hopes for reform.

————, *Gorbachev.* New York: Norton, 1986. An insightful look at the man who shut down the Soviet Union.

Bohdan Nahaylo and Victor Swoboda, *Soviet Disunion: A History of the Nationalities Problem in the USSR.* New York: Free Press, 1989. The nationalities problem started long before the formation of the Soviet Union, and the authors cover its history clearly.

Robert Payne, *The Life and Death of Lenin.* New York: Simon & Schuster, 1964. An excellent biography of the paradoxical world leader.

Richard Pipes, *The Russian Revolution.* New York: Knopf, 1990. Pipes is arguably the most authoritative historian of the Soviet Union writing today, as demonstrated by this essential study.

David Pryce-Jones, *The Strange Death of the Soviet Empire.* New York: Henry Holt, 1995. An interesting look at the decline of the Soviet Union. Pryce-Jones is a highly opinionated but well-respected writer who gives the facts and analyzes them very astutely.

Alexander Rabinowitch, *The Bolsheviks Come to Power.* New York: Norton, 1976. Not up to Pipes's or Chamberlin's standards, but still a very readable account of the revolution.

Francis B. Randall, *Stalin's Russia: An Historical Reconsideration.* New York: Free Press, 1965. In the 1960s historians began reexamining the Stalin era in light of information emerging during the Khrushchev era; an informative example of the revisionist trend.

Nicholas V. Riasanovsky, *A History of Russia.* 2nd ed. New York: Oxford University Press, 1969. Like Randall, Riasanovsky takes a fresh look at Russian history, especially the postrevolution era after Khrushchev.

Gail Sheehy, *The Man Who Changed the World: The Lives of Mikhail S. Gorbachev.* New York: HarperCollins, 1990. Sheehy, a popular writer, was fascinated by Gorbachev's personality and perhaps gives him more credit for shaping events than he deserves.

Hedrick Smith, *The Russians.* New York: Quadrangle, 1976. Smith was the *New*

York Times bureau chief in Moscow during much of the Brezhnev era. He writes of the lives of ordinary Russians and exposes the corruption endemic to that era.

Adam Ulam, *Stalin: The Man and His Era.* New York: Viking, 1973. Ulam is a somewhat sympathetic observer of Stalin, although he is capable of being critical; on the whole he presents a balanced picture of the Russian dictator.

Alexander Werth, *Russia: The Post-War Years.* New York: Taplinger, 1971. An interesting look at Russia since World War II.

Raymond E. Zickel, ed., *Soviet Union: A Country Study.* Washington, DC: Library of Congress, 1991. A useful reference work containing numerous statistics and analyses of the Soviet government, peoples, culture, and society; an excellent source for facts and figures.

Additional Works Consulted

Walter Adams et al., *Adam Smith Goes to Moscow: A Dialogue on Radical Reform.* Princeton, NJ: Princeton University Press, 1993.

William Barbour and Carol Wekesser, eds., *The Breakup of the Soviet Union.* San Diego: Greenhaven Press, 1994.

John Bergamini, *The Tragic Dynasty: A History of the Romanovs.* New York: G. P. Putman's Sons, 1969.

Ladislav Bittman, *The New Imagemakers: Soviet Propaganda and Disinformation Today.* Washington, DC: Pergamon-Brassey, 1988.

Arnaud de Borchgrave, "Ignoring Russia's Crisis of Crime," *Washington Times,* July 25, 1997.

Boris Leo Brasol, *The Balance Sheet of Sovietism.* New York: Duffield, 1922.

George William Buchanan, *My Mission to Russia.* New York: Arno Press, 1970.

Joel Carmichael, *A Cultural History of Russia.* New York: Weybright and Talley, 1968.

———, *A Short History of the Russian Revolution.* New York: Basic Books, 1964.

Fred Coleman, *The Decline and Fall of the Soviet Empire: Forty Years That Shook the World, from Stalin to Yeltsin.* New York: St. Martin's Press, 1996.

Timothy J. Colton and Robert Legvold, eds., *After the Soviet Union: From Empire to Nations.* New York: Norton, 1992.

Robert Conquest, *Stalin.* New York: Viking, 1991.

Robert V. Daniels, *Russia: The Roots of Confrontation.* Cambridge, MA: Harvard University Press, 1985.

Helene Carrere d'Encausse, *Lenin: Revolution and Power.* New York: Longman, 1982.

Sheila Fitzpatrick, *Stalin's Peasants: Resistance and Survival in the Russian Village After Collectivization.* New York: Oxford University Press, 1994.

Chrystia Freeland, "Russia Plans to Cut 200,000 State Jobs," *Financial Times,* March 25, 1998.

Mikhail Gorbachev, *The August Coup: The Truth and the Lessons.* New York: HarperCollins, 1991.

——— "New Truths and Political Realities" (speech given May 12, 1992), Green Cross International. http://web 243.petrel.ch/.

H. D. S. Greenway, "Gorbachev's Legacy," *Boston Globe,* December 27, 1991. http://homer.prod.oclc.org.

Adam Hochschild, *The Unquiet Ghost: Russians Remember Stalin.* New York: Viking, 1994.

George Frost Kennan, *American Diplomacy.* Chicago: University of Chicago Press, 1985.

———, *At a Century's Ending: Reflections, 1982–1995.* New York: Norton, 1996.

Victor Kravchenko, *I Chose Freedom: The Personal and Political Life of a Soviet Official.* New York: Scribner's, 1952.

Anatol Lieven, *Chechnya: Tombstone of Russian Power.* New Haven, CT: Yale University Press, 1998.

Richard Lourie, *Russia Speaks: An Oral History from the Revolution to the Present.* New York: E. Burlingame Books, 1991.

David Mandel, *The Petrograd Workers and the Fall of the Old Regime.* London: Macmillan Press, 1983.

Anatoly Marchenko, *From Tarusa to Siberia.* Royal Oak, MI: Strathcona, 1980.

Robert K. Massie, *Nicholas and Alexandra.* New York: Atheneum, 1967.

Peter J. Mooney, *The Soviet Superpower: The Soviet Union 1945–80.* London: Heinemann, 1982.

Jonathan Sanders, *Russia 1917: The Unpublished Revolution.* New York: Abbeville Press, 1989.

Index

Picture Credits

Cover photo: Corbis/Marc Garanger

Agence France Presse/Archive Photos, 65

AP/Wide World Photos, 57, 70, 71

Archive Photos, 17, 19, 21(both), 24, 27, 28, 29, 40, 50, 53, 58, 60, 61, 64, 68, 78

Archive Photos/Paris Match, 55

Bernard Gotfryd/Archive Photos, 67

Corbis, 33, 42, 43, 44, 47, 73

Fotokhronika Tass, 79, 82

FPG International, 15, 18, 26, 37(both), 51, 85, 93, 94

Imapress/Archive Photos, 72

North Wind, 12, 13

Novosti, 80, 84

Popperfoto/Archive Photos, 10, 39

Reuters/Michael Samojeden/Archive Photos, 87

Reuters/Rich Wilking/Archive Photos, 88

Reuters/Stringer/Archive Photos, 86

Reuters/Volodya Svartsevich/Archive Photos, 91

Stock Montage, Inc., 45

About the Author

John R. Matthews is the originating editor of *The World Wildlife Fund Guide to Endangered Species*. His books for young people include *Eating Disorders* and *The Beginning Entrepreneur*.